TIBETAN HEALING

TIBETAN HEALING

The Modern Legacy of Medicine Buddha

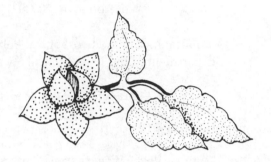

Peter Fenton

A publication supported by
THE KERN FOUNDATION

Quest Books
Theosophical Publishing House

Wheaton, Illinois ♦ Chennai (Madras), India

The Theosophical Publishing House
P.O. Box 270
Wheaton, IL 60189-0270

A publication of the Theosophical Publishing House,
a department of the Theosophical Society in America

Illustrations by Jean Herzel.

Illustration of Tara, page 185, courtesy Gelek Rinpoche. "How to prepare yourself
for a visit to a Tibetan Doctor," pages 108-12, used by permission from *Ayurvijnana*,
Vol. 5, No. 2, Autumn 1998. "Milarepa's Song," pages 158-9, used by permission
from Carol Publishing Group, 120 Enterprise Ave., Seacaucus, N.J. 07094.

Library of Congress Cataloging-In-Publication Data

Fenton, Peter.
Tibetan healing: the modern legacy of medicine Buddha / Peter
Fenton.
          p.   cm.
ISBN 0-8356-0776-3
1. Medicine, Tibetan.   2. Medicine, Buddhist.   3. Traditional
medicine.   I. Title.
R603.T5F53   1999
610'.951'5—dc21

                                                      99-16623
                                                      CIP

        5   4   3   2   1   *   99   00   01   02   03   04   05   06

Printed in the United States of America

FOR JEAN

Contents

Acknowledgments

For their enthusiasm and tireless support of this work, my deepest gratitude to the many medical people, fine scholars, and artists who helped illuminate even the most obscure points.

Among these are the lamas of Namgyal Monastery and the medical professionals of Men Tsee Khang who first introduced me to the Medicine Buddha tradition and revealed the vastness of its intellectual and spiritual architecture;

Lamas Yontan Gonpo and Inge Zangmo for their continuing friendship, guidance, and wisdom;

Brenda Rosen, who first championed and then edited this work;

John Sutton, for his continuing friendship and encouragement and for reminding me of what is truly important;

Madonna Gauding, who took the many diverse elements of this book and wove them seamlessly together;

Barbara Gerke, who made certain I met some of the most interesting and knowledgeable healers in West Bengal, who made significant contributions in terms of background research, and has been a friend throughout;

Professor Lama Chimpa, who not only put up with my incessant questioning but demonstrated, from time to time, his superiority at chess;

O. B. Dass, who escorted me throughout Kalimpong and into the Bengal Hills, moving ever more deeply into the heart of the local healing traditions;

Jim Ford, my neighbor and friend, who took two months from his busy life to photograph what we found in Nepal and India;

Jean Herzel, my wife and confidant, for her wonderful illustrations, sharp editorial suggestions, endless patience, and boundless good cheer.

Traditional Healing in a Modern World

I t is fortunate that mainstream culture is beginning, at last, to accept some of the wonderful ideas found in traditional methods of healing. This change of heart is hopeful for many reasons. Paramount is the fact that traditional healing offers us something we lack—specifically, a sane perspective on caring for our health. This situation is filled with irony since health care is what we in the West do best. We do it so well that it has become more than just a harmless preoccupation: unfortunately, it has become an unhealthy obsession.

Each new day brings an announcement of yet another "major medical breakthrough," another "miracle drug," another "surgical procedure." This seemingly endless tide of medical discoveries is supported by a zealous health-care industry seeking to capitalize on each advance. As a result, health care monopolizes much of our attention and consumes ever more of our resources. Many reasonable people feel that the time has come to take countermeasures and adopt a new health-care model. If we use care and discretion, we may find elements of a more balanced model in the traditional healing systems which are still relatively intact in the world's traditional cultures.

Some of these ancient systems are geared largely towards healing accidents or sudden illnesses. Others, much like our own system, prepare medications in anticipation of future difficulties. But despite great differences, most ancient traditions have a vital element in common—

the willingness to rely on spirit to aid the healing process.

The notion of spirit as a health transforming agent is conspicuously absent from modern medical practice. While a few courageous doctors have sought to reinstate prayer, meditation, visualization, and other spiritual practices as aids to healing, the majority, it seems, have neither the training nor the inclination to pursue practices that go beyond the accepted medical paradigm.

Conversely, in traditional cultures, spirit has always been a part of healing. In ancient and indigenous traditions and, until very recently, even in our own, there has never been any question that the health of the human body is intimately interconnected with the same spiritual forces responsible for our existence. In one way or another, this belief has enabled us to survive for millennia in the face of all challenges.

As we have lost the belief that our personal well-being is connected with the greater forces of the universe, so too we have lost the understanding that we are intimately linked with the natural world around us. Wherever it is found, this sense of connection translates into a concern, even a reverence for animate and inanimate nature. Today, however, we find ourselves so isolated from such ideas that it is even difficult to imagine how such a reverence might be expressed.

Gradually, we have let fundamental aspects of traditional human understanding slip away. We can no longer recall the songs or teaching stories of our ancestors. We know little or nothing of the actual practices that sustained us in times of need. We have difficulty distinguishing between the wide variety of healing herbs and plants often growing within our reach. We no longer know how to make or apply a simple poultice or gather herbs for a healing tea. Simply put, we have lost our healing heritage.

As a result, we have become increasingly reluctant to assume responsibility for the state of our own health. Instead, we have learned to

rely almost exclusively on advice from professionals—advice that we purchase. Healing knowledge is now largely the property of specialists and even of corporations, who regard health care as a business and not as a service to humanity. Perhaps we are just too busy, too harried by the demands of modern living to assume an added responsibility. Perhaps we have lost confidence in our ability to make wise health care choices. Whatever the reason, acceptance of responsibility for our own well-being would bring with it a special power. We would see ourselves and our environment with a deeper and refreshed insight. Reclaiming our healing wisdom might yet prove to be the salvation of humanity.

TIBETAN BUDDHISM AND MIND-BODY HEALING

Is it really possible to reclaim our heritage of healing wisdom? And if so, where can we turn for help?

At this moment in time, we have within our reach one of the world's great traditions of harmonious coexistence. Despite years of brutal suppression in its home country, Tibetan Buddhism now flourishes around the world carrying its message of nonviolence and absolute respect for all living beings. The Buddhist vision is one of immense scope and maturity. It includes within its protective embrace not only all people regardless of their beliefs but also all sentient beings, who, like ourselves, experience happiness and satisfaction, feel pain and suffering. Buddhism holds that all beings are subject to the same universal laws and respond to the same incentives and, for these reasons alone, are worthy of our care and compassion.

This same doctrine is found at the heart of Tibetan healing practice. Tibetan healing is a system of health care which bankrupts neither its patients nor the prevailing government. For the equivalent of a ten dollar bill, I received a half-hour diagnosis and a three-month supply of Tibetan medicine, representing some two hundred herbal pills of four different types. Of course, the treatment took place in India and

not in North America or Europe, where prices for all goods, including medicines, are high. But in its native environment, traditional Tibetan medical treatment, while not available to everyone, is certainly affordable by many.

The differences between such a system and our own are quite apparent. Patients of Tibetan healers do not receive organ transplants or brain scans. Nor is their blood generally sent to laboratories for analysis. But the absence of these specialized procedures does not necessarily mean failure. Many ailments are relieved. Even chronic and life-threatening problems, including, several of my informants told me, hepatitis and rabies, can be cured using traditional methods.

Time and again, Tibetans and others who rely on it extolled to me the potency of their healing techniques, which they claim to be superior in many ways to those of Western medicine. If these claims are true, then Westerners must ask the key question: why is this so?

Traditional Tibetan healing is based on principles far removed from our contemporary understanding of the body and its prerequisites for health. For instance, there is no escaping the fact that to understand Tibetan healing, it is first necessary to have some grasp of Buddhist concepts. This is true because the principles of Buddhism underlie the healing practices themselves.

Patients who understand these principles make it easier for the Tibetan doctor to explain why a new diet is recommended, for example, or new patterns of behavior are suggested. The best patient for this type of treatment is the one who works with the doctor in revealing these basic principles at work in the body. In a similar way, the best doctor is the one who encourages patients to participate at this level.

Moreover, the art of Tibetan healing involves the mind and spirit as much as the body. When I began my study of traditional Tibetan healing, its unqualified acceptance of the role of mind and spirit was what

attracted me most. Over time, the comprehensive body-mind-spirit philosophy of health drew me ever inwards, into my own nature as much as into the tradition.

I discovered, to my delight, that Tibetan healing is based on principles which apply to all of us equally—there are no exceptions, and there is only one route to robust health. By "robust," Tibetan healing implies more than just exceptional physical well-being. It also includes the notion of a stable and well-balanced mind. In fact, Tibetan healing is concerned first with the mind and only secondarily with the body. How this ordering of priorities is reflected in Tibetan healing practice is a central theme of this book.

LAMAS, SHAMANS, AND FOLK DOCTORS

Some Tibetan healing practices are performed only by Buddhist lamas—initiates who have spent much of their lifetime training their minds and refining their meditative skills. Many of these techniques are overtly spiritual in nature, involving prayer, meditation, and complex sacred rituals. Other methods, such as prescribing medication, diagnosis by pulse reading, or urinalysis, require a type of training similar in some respects to that of modern medical practitioners.

Today, as in the past, programs of medical study are taught to students in Buddhist monasteries and in other formal institutions designated especially as medical colleges. It is also common practice for traditional doctors to take on apprentices for a fee. In many cases, the apprentice is a young doctor in his "practical year." If the apprentice is a Tibetan Medical and Astrological Institute student, the fees are paid by the Institute. If the student is a relative of the doctor, the fees may be waived. Historically in Tibet, students presented the doctor to whom they apprenticed gifts such as gold and silver.

However, entirely separate healing methods exist outside formal

Buddhist institutions. These are the folk practices which often predate the Buddhist teaching institutions themselves. Family traditions, local experience and even, according to the practitioners themselves, the direct intervention of divine powers have all played a role in healing practices indigenous to the Himalayan region. Some of these techniques find their origins in Tibet, while others have arisen in nearby regions.

Folk healers and shamans cannot rightly be thought of in the same way as traditional Tibetan doctors. They have not had years of academic training and instruction in well-established institutions. Many employ methods based on a very different set of principles than those found in formal settings. Essentially, these practitioners believe that supernatural powers can be invoked both to inflict and to avert disease, misfortune, and calamities of all descriptions. In this sense, shamans are more closely allied to lamas who perform ritual exorcisms, for example, than they are to traditional Tibetan doctors who prescribe compounds. The ability to invoke spirits is often passed along family lines, and the art is not learned as such, but awakened.

Tibetan shamans have always played a great role in public health care. They do so even today and so should not be discounted as healing practitioners. Many shamanic traditions have remained virtually unchanged since ancient times. As such, they offer insight into the history and culture of the region and suggest ways in which certain more formal healing rituals might have developed. For these reasons, I have included in my discussion of Tibetan healing this exotic group of healers, who are very active in the region.

Tibetan doctors have historically been well respected in the Himalayan regions and, indeed, far beyond the boundaries of this mountain stronghold. Even today, it is well known that they are among the very best healers available. Sometimes these medicine people were sought out as teachers and summoned to distant lands at the request of emperors and maharajas. Common people, as well, sought out their services in times of need. Other methods having failed, these doctors were located, often with extreme difficulty and at great personal cost. Relatives

of a gravely ill or dying person realized they had little choice but to consult one of these elite practitioners. While conducting research for this book in India and Nepal, I became acquainted with a Sherpa tribesman who told me one such story involving his mother.

The Sherpas originally came from the higher altitudes in Nepal. In recent years, they have become well known for their abilities as porters during trekking expeditions. Their unexcelled reputation as mountain guides and for carrying heavy loads up and down mountain trails is well deserved, for they have become experts from centuries of practice. Sherpas have always engaged in trade with villagers in distant locations. Some, for example, in by-gone days, traveled hundreds of miles annually through unfamiliar jungles into India for this purpose.

In his entire life of nearly sixty years, Ang Kusang Sherpa had never seen a Sherpa doctor. Perhaps, he thought, they didn't exist. Tibetan doctors were a different story. They were well known to his people. When villagers from his home town of Namche fell ill, they would sometimes be taken into Tibet in the hope of finding such a healer. On other occasions, a Tibetan doctor would visit Ang's village. People from the surrounding area would then gather, and the doctor would conduct a clinic.

When we met, Ang Kusang Sherpa was the semi-retired owner of a Katmandu trekking company. He had spent the better part of his life working in a Tibetan refugee camp and hiking about the Himalayas. One day, in his beautiful house on the edge of Bodhnath, he told me the following story.

Ang Kusang Sherpa at his home in Bodhnath.

Ang Kusang Sherpa's Story

In our time, Peter, we didn't even know the main diseases. For nearly every problem we would say, "I have a cold." Even when we got headaches, we would say, "that's a cold." Sometimes, we would have stomach trouble as well. When we accidentally cut our hands or feet, we used a special herb, *khenpa*. We rubbed the juice right on the cut, and it would stop infections. It stopped the bleeding, too. Sometimes we would mix it with incense. But we didn't have any teas or know of any other special herbs.

When people did catch a cold, they were never allowed to sleep. Someone would always wait beside the sick person and wake them up. We believed that when a sick person slept, he caught additional diseases which were very, very bad. People who had headaches or fever or sweating were never allowed to sleep. I don't really know what the reason was for this, but as far as I remember, it happened in this way.

We had witch doctors and lamas, too. We depended on them completely. Even today we do. Not long ago a witch doctor was exorcising evil spirits from a woman. He beat her so badly that she died. Now this witch doctor is in prison.

There was a lama in our village, and every little place had its own monastery where people would pray. In our time, whenever there was sickness, we would always ask both the lama and the witch doctor to help. Both of them would try to combat it. The lama made *Mo* (divination) and then would tell us what was wrong. He would say, the sick person has this and that. Then he would tell us what to do, which *pujas* (ritual prayers) to say.

One time my mother was very sick. She got headaches all the time from carrying a little bit of firewood up the ladder to our living quarters. And she would get dizzy, too. We tried the witch doctor. We tried the lama.

The witch doctor and lama made pujas, but this didn't help. Then, after a while, we had to take her across the border into Tibet. At that time we had the yak to help us. Not all the yaks can be trained, but there is a special yak, born without horns. You find one or two of these out of every hundred. These are trained for carrying people on their backs. We put a horse saddle on them, and people can ride.

We didn't own the yak ourselves. If somebody needed a yak, they would just talk to the owner and then take it. In our time, everyone helped each other. It's different now. But then, we could use what other people had.

So my mother was carried by the yak into Tibet. There was just a trail. Every year it changed because of the glacier and avalanches. It was all stone and no forest, well above the tree line. From Namche into Tibet was about one week of traveling. There, we found a Tibetan doctor who helped her very much. He gave her Tibetan medical pills.

My father stayed with her, and after two months she felt much better. The system in Tibet worked like this: You had to keep the doctor very happy for the whole period. You had to give presents and things.

You know, not much has changed since then except that you can fly to Namche in a day. You should see it, Peter. You really should.

A CONCEPTUAL MAP OF TIBETAN MEDICINE

The easiest way to grasp the grand scheme of Tibetan medicine is to use a conceptual map. Fortunately, the Tibetans long ago realized the value of such a map as an instructional tool. Consequently, they invented one based on the information in their classical medical text, *The Four Medical Treatises* (more properly called *The Four Tantras.*). Known in Tibetan as *The Gyushi*, this book is believed to be the textual form of certain discourses of Shakyamuni Buddha, committed to writing by the Indian sage, Chandranandana sometime in the eighth century AD. These texts and their commentaries form the basis of an extraordinary set of paintings or *thangkas* which display the main ideas of Tibetan healing. Subjects include all categories of medical knowledge, such as history, philosophy, physiology, pathology, diagnosis, and treatment.

A *thangka* is a Tibetan painting which depicts ideas, personages, and historical or mythical events in iconographic form. These paintings have innumerable themes and are used for many purposes, including memorization, fact recall, and as aids to meditation.

The most famous medical thangkas are found illustrating a commentary on *The Gyushi* known as *The Blue Beryl* or *The Blue Lapis Lazuli*. This medical masterwork has seventy-six paintings containing more than ten thousand separate illustrations, each describing some aspect of Tibetan medicine. Created on the initiative of the Regent Sangye Gyamtso in the seventeenth century, the first edition of these paintings was used as an instructional tool and may have hung on the walls of the Chakpori Medical College in Lhasa, Tibet. At the turn of this century, an edition was sent by The Thirteenth Dalai Lama to Buryatia, in Siberia. The work was used as a reference by doctors trained in the Tibetan healing arts who were practicing in the region.

In 1936, during the Stalinist era of repression, the curator of the Buddhist Collection of the Museum of Atheism in Ulan-Ude, Buryatia, smuggled this unique collection from the Atsagat Monastery to the

museum for safekeeping. By 1958, the collection had been rediscovered in the Museum's archives, but a lack of funding kept most of the information it contained hidden from the public.

Perhaps the most interesting of all Tibetan medical illustrations are the thangkas which summarize the key points in the Tibetan healing system as elements of a giant tree. Known as the "Thangkas of the Medicine Trees," this great tree of healing has three root systems. One root system grows into a tree focused on the body. Its two trunks, twelve branches, eighty-eight leaves, two flowers, and three fruits depict both healthy and pathological body conditions. The tree which grows from the second or diagnostic root has three trunks. These correspond to the medical practices of observation, touch, and questioning. Its eight branches and thirty-eight leaves depict subdivisions of these diagnostic practices. The tree which grows from the third main root depicts various medical treatments. Its four trunks, twenty-seven branches, and ninety-eight leaves correspond to the four general types of prescriptions for changes in diet, behavior, medicine, and accessory treatments. A contemporary drawing of the Tree of Treatment appears here and on the cover of this book.

The Tibetan approach to organizing information is surprisingly contemporary. The characters and scenes on a thangka are actually icons designed specifically to elicit core ideas in the mind of the beholder. Further, these ideas are organized hierarchically. The high level of organization found in medical thangkas is a testament to the fine analytical skills of Tibetan artists and scholars.

Like the medical thangkas, the Tibetan medical texts themselves demonstrate that their authors knew the value of a systematic approach to classifying information. The first of *The Four Tantras*, for example, presents the chapter headings to be found in the subsequent three texts. In their first year of study, students memorize these chapter headings before learning any of the contents. In this way, they develop a cognitive structure which they later rely upon to retrieve more detailed information.

The thangka known as the Tree of Treatment works as an aid to memory. By studying it carefully, Tibetan healing practitioners are able to recall ideas related to the major divisions of treatment commonly used in Tibetan healing.

Whatever their human history, the source of the healing practices described by the medical thangkas and in *The Gyushi* itself is believed ultimately to be the Buddha. Tibetan tradition holds that one of the manifestations of the historical Buddha of our era, Shakyamuni or Siddhartha Gautama, born about 500 BC, was the Medicine Buddha. Tradition has it that from each of the Medicine Buddha's psychic centers, a separate Buddha appeared to teach one of the four treatises which comprise *The Gyushi*. The first of these, Amitabha, sprang from the Buddha's throat and made a request for the subsequent teachings. In response, four more Buddhas appeared in succession. Akshobhya originated from Medicine Buddha's heart center and taught the first, or Root Tantra. Vairochana sprang from his crown and taught the second or Explanatory Tantra. Ratnasambhava came from the navel and taught the third or Oral Tradition Tantra; while Amoghasiddhi came from the secret region or root chakra and presented the fourth or Last Tantra. Each of these Buddhas is an emanation of the same great being.

COMBINING WESTERN AND TRADITIONAL HEALING

In many parts of the world, including Asia as I discovered, one of the most startling sights is the number of people walking about with severe, obviously untreated diseases. More unsettling still is the knowledge that for just a few dollars, many of these problems could be cured or at least allayed. Some of these diseases can be successfully

Each leaf illustrates a specific medical suggestion for particular diseases believed to be caused by imbalances among the three humors known as wind, bile, and phlegm. A leaf on the branch related to behavior, for example, suggests that patients with wind disorders be surrounded by joyful, well-wishing friends. On the branch related to diet, a leaf suggests that patients with bile disorders take warm water. The limb of the medications branch relating to wind disorders devotes several leaves to describing soup therapies. The branch of alternate therapies has several leaves devoted to phlegm disorders. One of these suggests moxibustion treatment, the practice of burning substances on or over specific acupuncture points.

treated with traditional healing practices, while others, such as leprosy, can only be arrested, it seems, by Western procedures.

With a pantheon of Buddhas such as these to inform Tibetan healing practice, it is not surprising that the sacred lies at its heart.

Curiously, in researching this book, I did notice something of a melding of Eastern and Western medical cultures, or at least a willingness on the part of medical people of both traditions to explore new possibilities. Perhaps it is the realization of the magnitude of the problem—ever greater numbers of people requiring immediate attention—that has brought about this willingness by healers of all persuasions to accommodate foreign ideas. Perhaps, too, it is something of an admission that valuable medical knowledge may indeed lie outside the scope of traditional practices. This openness to change and exploration seems to be true, in Asia at least, not only of methods for diagnosis and treatment but also at the more fundamental levels of medical research and long-term record keeping of patient information.

I found unmistakable evidence of this merging of traditions at one health center in Bodhnath, Nepal, where the possibilities for the future were very clearly on display. A Western-style allopathic doctor would work in the clinic on one day, and a Tibetan doctor on another. Between the doctors' visits, either Western nurses or Tibetan nuns would care for patients. The medicines from each tradition were organized on the shelves by type, with Tibetan on one side, Western on the other.

In a different setting, I watched Tibetan lamas and nuns working side by side with an allopathic doctor dispensing both Western and traditional medicine. How heartening it was to see this cooperation. It renewed my faith in the ability of professionals to work together despite vast differences in culture and training. It was also reassuring to see professionals addressing the urgent situation of public health.

His Holiness the Dalai Lama recently expressed similar sentiments at an international congress for Tibetan medicine. In a presentation entitled, "The Relevance of Tibetan Medicine to the West," he said, "I believe that Tibetan medicines must be appreciated in scientific terms, in terms of their constitutive elements—be they herbal, mineral, precious stones, metal, bones . . . . I believe that Tibetan medicine should be considered a distinct science from ritual. Rituals and mantras can be complimentary, but the fact remains that Tibetan medicine should be useful, is useful, to those without any intent or inclination to the spiritual side." This statement suggests that the Dalai Lama has confidence in the public health value of Tibetan medicine even without its spiritual practices and encourages its investigation from that standpoint.

This wall of medicines, some Tibetan and some Western, symbolizes the hope that in the future both traditions will strengthen their relationship in the field of health care. As we are now finding out, there is much to be gained from a greater exchange of ideas.

Recent writings by Tibetan medical doctors also confirm this willingness to investigate their healing practices from a scientific point of view. Indeed, many are making every effort to do so. Given the current interest in the West about the Tibetan pharmacopoeia, there is little doubt that the future will find these two approaches to health care working together more closely still.

The Book of the Dead

My adventure with Tibetan ideas began nearly thirty years ago when a strange and wonderful book came my way. It did not fit with philosophy, literature, history, or science, so I placed it in a special section of my library—with books I somehow associated with "mysticism." These books were my favorites, forbidden and dark though they sometimes seemed.

The book was entitled *The Tibetan Book of the Dead or The After-Death Experiences on the Bardo Plane.* What could it be about, I wondered? In adolescent haste, I skipped the numerous prefaces, lengthy commentaries, foreword, and introduction, and began with Chapter One. Not very far into the book, I realized with growing excitement that it was a kind of map. Properly understood, it was intended to prepare a person for the dying process and offered instructions on successfully navigating the after-death realm towards a higher state of consciousness or, at least, into a favorable rebirth.

The Tibetan Book of the Dead

O nobly-born (so-and-so by name) the time hath now come for thee to seek the path (in reality). Thy breathing is about to

cease. Thy guru hath set thee face to face before the Clear Light; and now thou art about to experience it in its Reality in the Bardo state, wherein all things are like the void and the cloudless sky, and the naked, spotless intellect is like unto a transparent vacuum without circumference or center. At this moment, know thou thyself; and abide in that state. I, too, at this time, am setting thee face to face.[1]

A thousand questions filled my mind: Who wrote this guidebook? How did its authors know what happens after death? What is the Clear Light? Do dying people really encounter it? Nothing I had read in Western philosophy or psychology had prepared me for such ideas. Neither did my religious background supply much useful information. I was thrilled by the idea that someone knew enough about the hereafter to write down a clear description of what to expect when we die, as well as detailed instructions about how to prepare for death.

The Buddha as physician, dharma as medicine, and sangha as nurse can help us lead healthier, more balanced lives.

THE SPIRITUAL MEDICINE OF THE DHARMA

Eventually I discovered that Tibetan philosophy, even treatises for the dead and dying, were in essence high-level Tibetan healing practices. Although it would seem that there is little point in administering medicine to the dead, what seems to be dying in one realm may very well be awakening into another. At least, so stated *The Book of the Dead*.

Moreover, the medicine *The Book of the Dead* obliges us to administer to the dying is more spiri-

tual than physical. According to Buddhist teachings, the most potent medicine available to cure the ills of this life and of the life to come is the *dharma*, the teachings of the Buddha. By following the prescriptions of the dharma, we learn essential truths about ourselves and our human condition. This knowledge helps us sort out what is really important and choose consciously how we live and how we die. Further, we learn that there are steps we can take to avoid rebirth into one of the more unpleasant realms of existence; the most important of these steps is being of genuine service to others.

This approach made eminent sense to me. Wise preparation for death is actually, I realized, a prescription for living. By facing the inevitability of our own death and the deaths of those we love—unpleasant thoughts that we generally put out of our minds—we learn to take the best advantage of the life we have. Facing death helps us recognize that personal happiness is only one measure of life's success. As we contemplate our own impermanence and the impermanence of every being and everything in this world, we discover ways to conduct our daily affairs so as to bring maximum benefit to ourselves and to the world around us.

A traditional Buddhist analogy underscores this message. It holds that the Buddha is the doctor who prescribes what will help in life and in death. The dharma is both the Buddha's teachings and the spiritual development that takes place in us as we put the powerful medicine of the teachings to work in our lives. The *sangha*, or community of Buddhist practitioners, is the nurse, our companions on the path, who comfort and care for us as we struggle to heal from the physical and emotional ills that are inherent

For those who can recognize them, omens can be found everywhere, in dreams or in waking states. Dreams of the great deities, of swimming across a large body of water, of riding an elephant or lion are all signs of health and prosperity. On the other hand, dreams of riding a monkey or of being swallowed by a great fish herald the most unfortunate of circumstances, one's impending death.

in this life. Collectively, Budddha, dharma, and sangha are called the Three Jewels. They are the true remedy, Buddhists believe, for the ills and woes of the world.

THE IDEA OF REINCARNATION

On the surface, at least, the Tibetan perspective on death seems not so very different from the Western view. Here is a description of a Tibetan death procession that took place early in this century: "White *khadas* (ceremonial scarves) are wrapped around his body and the single khada held by the priest walking ahead and tied to the corpse is to guide him on the White Path so that he may not stray on to the Black Path that leads to hell. He will be cremated a little farther along the valley, and tonight his soul will be led by the demons that inhabit the cremation grounds to Shenji, the Ruler of the Dead, where he will be judged. Om Mani Padme Hum! May all sentient beings find their goal. We must all go the same way one day."[2]

The funeral described above seems neither excessively strange nor filled with indecipherable rituals. With a few slight changes, the scene might have taken place in the West. The idea of Judgment Day is well understood in the Judeo-Christian worldview. But just below the threshold of the visible, the beliefs of the people in the procession are governed by an extraordinary doctrine. For millions of people, including Tibetans, reincarnation is a living reality, no more to be doubted than the fact that the sun rises and sets. Unlike the Christian afterlife which is described as eternal, the next world into which the reincarnated dead awaken is no more permanent than this one. It is simply another life–in hell, as an animal, as a human, or even in one of the "god realms," which Westerners might term "heaven." There, the being which carries the continuation of the mind stream of our present life lives out a new one, eventually to die again and again to be reborn.

The principle governing this cycle is called karma. *Karma* is simply

the law of cause and effect. Every thought, word, or deed of every living being creates a karmic cause, the effects of which will manifest either in this life or in some future life. Through karma's inexorable mechanism, all beings are born and reborn into the most suitable life, one which specifically matches their state of development and perfectly reflects their deeds and misdeeds. Good actions lead to positive results, including fortunate rebirth in the human or god realms. Bad actions lead to negative results, including rebirth as a hell being or an animal.

There is no escaping the effects of karmic law save through awakening to its inevitability and living one's life so as to create the karmic causes for a positive future. Until we do, karma governs us. As we become conscious and aware, our thoughts and behavior change in positive new directions. As a direct consequence, our health and worldly circumstance improve. A favorable rebirth, it is said, will afford us the opportunity to consolidate and actually increase these gains.

For Tibetan Buddhists, the concept of an afterlife, indeed, a seemingly infinite number of afterlives, is fundamental. To help beings navigate these apparently endless spans of time, Buddhists have developed an elaborate timeline. They recognize two types of time: Historical time relates to events in known human history. Cosmological time locates events on a superhuman scale. The historical person we know as Siddhartha Gautama, or Shakyamuni Buddha, for example, is Buddha's manifestation for this current immeasurably long period of time. He is said to have begun his journey toward Buddhahood under the tutelage of Buddha Dipankara many eons ago. After countless lives in many forms—some of the Buddha's animal lifetimes are recounted in the charming Jataka Tales—his reign will end—accounts differ as to the precise date—and the Buddha Maitreya will succeed him.

Like Shakyamuni, we and all living beings have the capacity to progress in acquiring compassion and wisdom until, like these great Buddhas, we truly understand our own nature. When this happens, we are liberated from ordinary states of consciousness and gain access to

the infinitely heightened awareness known as enlightenment. Until such a time, we continue to cycle in a continuous chain of birth and rebirth. Its links are forged by our thoughts, words, and deeds, products of our unenlightened state of mind. Essentially, we must think of ourselves as ill and regard the "symptom" of our illness to be an endless chain of reincarnations. In its fundamental character, health is the compassionate and wise state of mind that makes enlightenment possible.

THE THREE MIND POISONS

Rig-pa is a Tibetan word which refers to mind in its primordial state: pristine, shining, unobstructed, enlightened. The prefix *ma* indicates that a quality is not present. Thus the term *ma-rig-pa* suggests unenlightened mind and its consequence, a less than perfect state of health. The ideas conveyed by the terms *rig-pa* and *ma-rig-pa* are not only crucial to understanding Buddhism but are also platform concepts which underlie Tibetan healing practices.

Ma-rig-pa is often defined simply as "ignorance." But in Buddhist philosophy, ignorance is not merely a state of "not knowing"; it is a state of "wrong knowing," characterized by thought processes which are deluded or obscured and consequently reflect only a limited awareness of the true nature of reality. Buddhist philosophy holds that the world that we see and believe to be "real" is, in fact, an illusion. Though we think the objects and people we see, including ourselves, exist solidly from their own sides, they are, seen rightly, no more substantial than dreams or, as it is often expressed poetically, than the reflection of a moon in a clear lake.

Moreover, the self which we cherish and protect is likewise a fiction. Though we and all beings of this world exist "relatively," and thus can perform all the actions and routines of our everyday life, we are not the stable and fixed entities we seem to be when we thump our chests and say, "It's me." Our true nature is more like an ever-changing

process, a series of dependent relationships of cause and effect, which arise, moment to moment, as a result of causes created in the previous moments of our existence.

More than an unfortunate state of mind, *ma-rig-pa* has consequences. Simply put, it is not healthy to be ignorant. Ignorance gives rise to two lesser poisons, aversion and attachment. These three "mind poisons" are often represented by animal symbols: the black hog symbolizes ignorance; the green snake, aversion, and the red cock, attachment. Sometimes these creatures are shown biting each other's tails, which represents their intimate and functional interconnection.

Moreover, as well as affecting our minds, the poisons also affect our bodies. Modern medical science is well aware of these effects. Excessive attachment to food, drink, and other indulgences is often cited by medical researchers as root causes of disease. Attachment to alcohol, sugar, tobacco, and fat, for instance, is linked to everything from diabetes to heart disease and cancer. Aversion to positive routines such as regular exercise is similarly pointed to as a cause of weakness, deterioration, or illness. In its more severe form, aversion manifests as hatred and uncontrolled anger, a commonly cited cause of high blood pressure and stroke.

THE WHEEL OF LIFE

The cycle of uncontrolled rebirths which arise as a result of karma is depicted by a symbolic drawing called the "Wheel of Life." At the center of the wheel are the hog, snake, and cock, which represent the mind poisons. Cycling around them are the six realms of existence

Ignorance, aversion, and attachment are described as "poisons" because they work to destroy or prevent the insights our minds would generate in a healthier state. Like an infernal machine at the core of unenlightened existence, the three encourage, nourish, and irritate one another. Working in consort, they condition the mind and consequently the behavior of sentient beings. All other negative states of mind are seen as arising from their influence. In this way, Tibetan philosophy postulates the link, in the form of disease, between mind and matter.

where beings propelled by karma take rebirth.

The higher realms are those of humans, jealous gods, and gods. The lower realms include those of the animals, hungry ghosts, and hell be-

ings. Each of these domains is characterized by affinities to certain afflictions. The human realm, for example, is rooted in creative activity and in pride and passion, while that of the hungry ghosts is centered around greed and insatiability. The god realm is noted for its carefree character, and its inhabitants are devoted to a life of aesthetic pleasure. This realm is often depicted with its beings singing, dancing, or playing musical instruments. Opposing this is a hell realm every bit as terrifying as the Christian version, where beings continuously endure horrific, merciless torture.

It should be noted that the punishments of the various realms are not inflicted on us by an omnipotent God in response to our crimes. Rather, they are natural results which have arisen in response to the karma generated by our thoughts, words, and deeds. Afflictions such as disease, accident, and misfortune arise as direct consequences of negative karma. As a Buddhist maxim states: "We are not punished for our sins, but by them."

Since the Wheel of Life has neither beginning nor end, it suggests the eternal cycle of death and rebirth. Around the representations of the three mind poisons and the six realms of existence are a set of images called the Twelve Links. These represent the chain of causality which propels us from life to life.

As has been noted, neither the fortunate nor unfortunate realms represent a permanent state of being. When their negative karma has been exhausted, hell beings die and are reborn, perhaps as humans or gods if they have sufficient positive karma to propel them upward in the

scheme. Likewise, when their positive karma has been used up, even gods can be reborn into a hell-realm existence.

These realms, including our human realm, are created through the cause-and-effect mechanism of our limited awareness. Since they are sustained by imperfect states of mind, they are considered to be depen-dent and ultimately illusory. As our knowledge and awareness increase, the illusions surrounding these seemingly solid states of being be-gin to fall away. Until we reach these higher states of mind, however, we are confined to existence in these pseudo-worlds characterized by suffering and dissatisfaction.

With proper instruction, it is pos-sible to stop our endless cycling around the Wheel of Life and achieve liberation. Buddhist meditation training teaches one to recognize the progressive states of dying so that one can aim for the Clear Light. This spe-cial light occurs naturally during the dying process and points the way off the wheel and out of *samsara*, the cycle of uncontrolled rebirths propelled by karma. However, until all negative karma attached to our consciousness is appeased, our attraction towards re-birth is too powerful to avoid. After a

According to The Tibetan Book of the Dead, af-ter dying, the indestructible essence of a per-son still exists in a Bardo, a state somewhere between life and death. This essence is quite con-scious though purely mental in formation. In fact, it is understood to be far more intelligent than a nor-mal human consciousness.

period of generally no more than forty-nine days in the *Bardo*, or in-between state, a being is eventually drawn toward rebirth in one of the six realms. Thus life itself is seen as a condition of disease, the only cure for which is the absolute and effortless wisdom of enlightenment.

CHAPTER TWO

A Medicine Buddha Retreat

Ithaca, New York, seemed a long way from my forest home in the Cabinet Mountains of Idaho. But this particular year, Ithaca held a special attraction. A team of experts on Tibetan healing, members of Men Tsee Khang, the Medical and Astrological Institute of His Holiness the Dalai Lama, would be coming from Dharamsala, India, to conduct an eight-day retreat. In addition to an overview of the Tibetan medical tradition, they would be giving an initiation into ritual aspects of the practice. Always eager to learn more about traditional forms of healing, I quickly made arrangements to attend.

A few weeks later, I found myself face to face with "Medicine Buddha," as the Tibetan healing tradition is called. The title indicates how closely Tibetan medicine is allied to spiritual affairs. In fact, the relationship is intimate, since Buddhist philosophical ideas provide much of the underlying theory for the medical practice itself.

The Venerable Khensur Rinpoche, the formidable abbot and senior resident teacher of Ithaca's Namgyal Monastery, would preside personally over our Medicine Buddha initiation.

Khensur Rinpoche assumed his throne each morning and began the day with a lecture on a topic of relevance to Tibetan healing practice.

Since Namgyal is the seat of His Holiness the Dalai Lama in North America, Khensur Rinpoche's position is lofty indeed. Distinguished as the past abbot of the parent Namgyal Monastery in Dharamsala, India, he had received teachings and initiations in each of the four main traditions of Tibetan Buddhism. He is also a renowned scholar and lecturer.

As with all ritual initiations, the empowerment of Medicine Buddha can only be conferred by a lama who has received the initiation. Khensur Rinpoche had received the initiation from many qualified teachers, including the current Dalai Lama himself and those who had taught him.

The Namgyal Tree

As is the case with many Tibetan terms, the word *Namgyal* is associated with an interesting story. Namgyal is a mythical tree with incredible powers of healing. More commonly known as the "Completely Victorious Myrobalan," this miraculous tree no longer grows in our realm because of the "degenerate" nature of our current age. Here is its story:

Namgyal was originally planted in the realm of the gods by Yitrogma, an emanation of the goddess Dusolmah. By praying to the Buddhas of four directions, Yitrogma was able to discover the tree's remarkable healing abilities. In addition to its physical healing properties, Namgyal can cleanse wrongdoings, remove mental obscurations, impart long life, bring wealth and good fortune, and even make the body indestructible. These sacred qualities are depicted in thangka paintings of Medicine Buddha. In his right hand, the Buddha holds a branch of Namgyal.

Altogether, there are five types of Myrobalan trees. Four of these, known as Golden, Kempo, Longsih, and the Myrobalan of Seven Foldings, are still used as ingredients in medicines. Even the essence of the fifth, Namgyal, can still be procured from the spiritual dimension through the blessings of Medicine Buddha. The essence is stored in his offering bowl which he holds in his left hand. It will infuse any medicine, including medicine made from the other Myrobalan plants, with special healing qualities.[3]

BE LAMPS UNTO YOURSELVES

Each morning, the Abbot seated himself cross-legged on his teaching "throne" placed several feet above the audience. The throne was actually a simple cushion resting on a wooden box painted red. Also on the box was a small table covered with colorful scarves. On this, the lama had arranged the ritual objects he would use for the initiation and a vase of freshly cut flowers.

Among the objects were two which caught my attention immediately—an ornate hand bell about six inches tall and a curiously shaped double-pointed scepter called a *vajra* or *dorje* about four inches long.

*V*ajra, or diamond scepter, is a Sanskrit term which originally referred to the fearsome weapon of Indra, the consummate male deity of ancient India. Buddhists have reversed its meaning, preferring instead to regard the supreme universal force as the infinite compassion and skillful methods of helping known to a Buddha. The dorje, held in the lama's right hand, also represents the masculine principle.

The feminine counterpart of the dorje is the bell. It symbolizes blissful wisdom of the true nature of reality. Held in the lama's left hand, it is rung at the level of his heart. Near the top of the bell's handle is a small face, said by some to represent Prajnaparamita, the goddess of wisdom.

Many among those of us assembled for the initiation were seated comfortably on the floor on mats or meditation cushions. The rest sat on chairs arranged in a semicircle at the back. Surrounding us, on the walls and on tables, were the objects I had come to associate with Vajrayana Buddhism.

Three thangkas and a picture of the Dalai Lama hung on the wall beside the throne. Closest to the throne was an image of White Tara, a gentle goddess known for her powers of healing and her infinite mercy and compassion. The middle thangka depicted Shakyamuni Buddha seated in the lotus position. An orange moon disk floated behind his head. The third thangka was an image of Medicine Buddha, blue in color, with a green moon disk shining behind his head. Slightly higher than the thangkas hung a portrait of the Dalai Lama, illuminated at the base by two small lights.

An altar was set up in front of the thangkas. It held a vase of peacock feathers, bowls of fruit and other food offerings, and several burning butter lamps. On some days, *tormas* (ritual cakes), elaborate butter sculptures of goats, elephants, and monkeys, bowls of rice, and delicious pastries were placed there as additional offerings.

Ritual Offerings

In Tibetan tradition, every home has an altar. Here, offerings are presented to the Three Jewels: Buddha, Dharma, and Sangha. The Three Jewels are represented on the altar by a statue or thangka painting, sacred texts or dharma books, and ritual objects such as a bell and dorje.

Each day, offerings such as seven bowls of water, fruit, flowers, and candles or butter lamps are placed in front of the images. The offerings symbolize the practitioner's respect for the teachers, the teachings, and the community of practitioners. Through meditation, the practitioner envisions that whatever offerings have been arranged have become perfectly pure, have been transformed into nectar, and are infinite in quantity.

The person making the offerings also abandons any thought of immediate, personal benefit. Instead, the offerings are regarded as symbols of profound respect and limitless generosity. During meditation, it is imagined that the Three Jewels and all enlightened beings rejoice in the offerings, which bring them happiness and joy.

Rinpoche began the retreat with a warning: "We should not blindly follow the teachings of the Medicine Buddha. We must consider. We have to acquire everything by ourselves and not depend on others." Very clearly, this was an injunction for each of us to use our own analytical

abilities in pursuit of the truth about Tibetan healing practices. How refreshing, I thought. Here was a medical tradition that encouraged laypeople to investigate carefully the precepts on which it is based. How extraordinarily different from medical practice in the West!

We were being asked to form our own opinions about the Medicine Buddha teachings. This suggested, ultimately, that we were personally responsible for whatever we learned. Was this level of personal responsibility, I wondered, characteristic of all of the dharma teachings?

As his own death approached, Buddha Shakyamuni had reminded his disciples that "Everything that is compounded will decay." With this simple statement, he made clear that our judgments, like all other productions of human consciousness, are not permanent. Everything we believe or hold dear will someday be lost. But to console his followers, the Buddha added, "Be lamps unto yourselves," suggesting that they seek to become independent and self-reliant.

As the eight-day retreat unfolded, two doctors and an astrologer from Men Tsee Khang and several monks and the abbot of Namgyal outlined a complex system of interrelationships between mind, our understanding of the nature of reality, and disease. The concepts presented ranged from the simple to the overwhelmingly complex. Some I found eminently believable, while others seemed utterly fantastic. As I sat and listened, I reflected on the Buddha's advice on independent and responsible thinking and found it very helpful.

The most difficult task for me was sorting out what I had previously regarded as "medical" information from what I thought of as "spiritual" information. I soon gave up. In the Medicine Buddha tradition, drawing such lines was impossible. We heard lectures on such doctrinal topics as the three principle aspects of the Buddhist path, the seven-point system of training the mind to realize perfect compassion, and the four types of tantra. We also heard presentations on such topics related to specific rituals, such as the uses of mantra, visualization

practice, and making *tormas* or ritual cakes. Specifically medical talks covered collecting and preparing medicinal plants, the humors, treating patients using behavior, diet, and meditation, and the relationship between Tibetan astrology and healing.

My sense of being overwhelmed by all of this, I discovered, was not unique. In fact, some Tibetan doctors admit that mastering all aspects of this complex discipline is nearly impossible. As Dr. Lobsang Wangyal expressed it: "All my speculations about Tibetan medicine changed gradually as I began my studies. I later became convinced of its sound, systematic, and logical framework. My appetite to learn Tibetan healing grew since then, until I finally came to realize that I would not be able to learn everything about Tibetan medicine in one lifetime."[4]

After musing over this predicament for some time, I remembered the idea of reincarnation, and my intellectual horizons opened, just a little. What if I had several lifetimes to master the intricacies of Tibetan healing? Though it is said that most of us forget the specifics of what we have learned in one lifetime during the passage into the next, surely it would be easier to learn it all again, going further and deeper the next time around. I was beginning to lose preconceived ideas that had been holding me back. This change, I realized with a jolt, was due to the medicine of the dharma.

As it turned out, however, my newly discovered openness would soon be put to the test by the Medicine Buddha initiation itself.

MEDICINE BUDDHA INITIATION

The initiation began with saffron water poured into our cupped hands. By drinking it, we symbolically purified our mouths. We then made a formal request to the lama to bestow the initiation.

The Story of the Vase Blessing and the Butter Offering

As the blessing water was passed around, there was some concern that there might not be enough for everyone. This prompted Paldin, the translator, to tell a story:

A monk from Kham, a region in eastern Tibet, had traveled a long distance to Lhasa, in the central part of the country, to receive a long life empowerment from a certain lama. Now this person had a slab of butter. He thought, when I receive the empowerment, I will offer this butter to the lama.

Great numbers of pilgrims arrived from different regions, so there was quite an assembly. When the lama gave this initiation, he usually touched each member of the assembly on the head with a special vase. But, because he was older, he did not have the strength to touch everyone. He could only touch the people directly in front of him.

When this point in the ritual was reached, the lama said, "For those of you I have not touched with this vase, just imagine that I have done so."

The pilgrim from Kham was in the very last row and so was not touched personally by the lama. Having traveled such a great distance, he was disappointed. When it came time to give offerings to the lama, he said, "If I must imagine receiving your touch, you must imagine receiving my butter."

Rinpoche then explained that the only appropriate motivation for receiving an initiation is *bodhicitta*, the intention to seek enlightenment so as to be able effortlessly to benefit living beings. Such altruistic motivation is the central principle of Mahayana Buddhism. A practitioner on this path vows to become a Buddha and then to return to life in this realm until every living creature has achieved the goal of liberation from suffering.

The Mahayana path is further divided, we learned, into two sets of teachings, *sutra* and *tantra*. Both teachings originated with the Buddha himself. Sutra teachings help us realize the impermanent, suffering nature of this life. Further, they outline the stages of practice and realization necessary to achieve liberation. Tantra imparts the "quick and dangerous" method of reaching enlightenment within a short time—even this very lifetime. The Medicine Buddha practice falls into the category of tantra. Thus initiation from a qualified lama is a prerequisite to practice.

In their capacity as Namgyal monks, the Venerables Tenzin Yignyen, Tenzin Lhawang, and Tenzin Legdin assisted in many ways during the next eight days.

EMPTINESS

The most profound philosophical concept Rinpoche explained was the notion of *shunyata*, commonly known as "emptiness." He was forceful in his insistence that this idea is critical both to Buddhist practice in general and the Medicine Buddha practice in particular.

According to my understanding, which is doubtlessly flawed, emptiness describes the authentic way everything in the world exists. Our minds tend to see things around us, and even ourselves, as solid and unchanging. We perceive these things as having an intrinsic reality—a

valid status as independent and autonomous creations. Viewing the world in this way is our delusion.

According to the theory of emptiness, everything that exists, including ourselves, actually lacks this intrinsic existence. Whatever we encounter in the world is really "empty" of the "reality" or "truth status" we assign to it. The things and beings—even our cherished self—are nothing more than images dancing in an ever-shifting play of appearances that arise in our deluded consciousness.

Understanding emptiness from an intellectual standpoint is not the same thing as realizing it in meditation. When, through deep reflection, we begin to recognize the true nature of reality, we see that everything, including our minds, has an original, unaffected state. This condition is often described as primordial, empty, and luminous.

Until we come face to face with the original nature of our minds, all our perceptions will be imperfect. We will struggle with the mistaken sense that there is a separation between self and other, subject and object, knower and known. We will be trapped by the elaborate conceptual framework we create and constrained to work within its strictures rather than enjoying the freedom and brilliance of natural wisdom.

In terms of healing work, it is helpful to remember that the separation we perceive between sickness and health, patient and healer, symptom and medicine are also "empty" of intrinsic reality. The constant stream of conditions which comprises "reality" can place us directly in touch with any problem or situation. Recognizing this stream and learning to use it enables us to bridge any perceived gap and to understand any situation more fully. In this way, we can achieve the freedom to bring about radiant health and well-being in ourselves and in others.

In the Realm of the Medicine Buddha

As the initiation ceremony unfolded, I realized that my task as I sat there was to visualize, or imagine in my mind's eye, the realm of the Medicine Buddha as the lama described it to us. Rinpoche began by asking us to visualize our immediate surroundings—an Elk's assembly hall—as the Pure Land of Medicine Buddha, a mystical country whose substance is pristine awareness.

Populating this imaginary country were spiritual heroes and heroines, various protectors and guardians, and the eight Medicine Buddhas themselves, dressed in colorful robes. The offerings of fruit and flowers on the altar were transformed, in our imaginations, into pure and luminous gifts, worthy of presenting to these great beings. Slowly, with great concentration, we created a detailed psychic landscape.

Following recitations and prayers, we were asked to visualize a lotus flower, the center of which was a white moon disk, floating just above the crowns of our heads. On this lotus throne, set with jewels and precious stones, we envisioned the radiant Medicine Buddha, translucent and blue, holding a lapis lazuli bowl overflowing with healing nectar in his left hand and a branch of the Myrobalan tree, king of medicinal plants, in his right.

The Medicine Buddha holds the King of Medicine Plants, the Myrobalan, in his right hand and his offering bowl, filled with healing nectar, in the left.

Until we were asked to take the "Bodhisattva Vow," I had managed to keep

up with the visualization. Now, however, I encountered a snag of monumental proportions. There is nothing really complicated about this vow. Simply put, you pledge to postpone personal liberation until every sentient being—bugs, birds, animals, people—becomes free of suffering, that is, until they attain enlightenment. The quest is noble and full of love for all creation. Nevertheless, the time frame involved made me extremely uncomfortable.

At the very moment when I should have taken the vow, I found I could not. Instead, my thoughts flashed back to a time several years earlier. I had been chatting with a youthful employee of a Tibetan bookstore. She mentioned, with a knowing, confident smile, that she had taken the Bodhisattva Vow. I wondered then if she had any idea how long liberating all sentient beings might take. How could she, I asked myself, or any of us, make a commitment that stretched seemingly to eternity? I had never resolved this question and so, saddened and confused, I hesitated, stumbled, and fell. In so doing, I missed my chance.

Fortunately, I had less difficulty with the next part of the initiation, reciting the mantra of Medicine Buddha. As we recited the mantra, we imagined that infinite rays of white light poured down from the Medicine Buddha above our heads, completely filling and purifying our bodies, leaving them as clean and clear as crystal.

Like most mantras, the mantra of Medicine Buddha is preserved in Sanskrit. Its translation is something like: "Homage to the Highly Realized Lapis Lazuli Healing Guru Medicine Buddha, to the Great Realized Ones, Homage to the Healing, to the Healing, to the Supreme Healing. So Be It."

We continued to recite the mantra, imagining as we did so that healing rays of pure and brilliant light radiated outwards from Medicine Buddha to all sentient beings, carrying with them the love and compassion of all the enlightened beings, purifying them of diseases, afflictions, negative karma, and ignorance.

We concluded by imagining Medicine Buddha dissolving into light and then absorbing into our hearts. Now I found myself afflicted with remorse. Since I had not given myself wholeheartedly to the Bodhisattva Vow, I felt like an interloper. Still, I was not about to give up. I had been told to discover for myself the truth about Tibetan healing practices, and this I was determined to do.

Blessing the Medicine

One of the most interesting aspects of the Medicine Buddha practice is its use as a means to bless medicines. In many parts of the world, it is believed that blessing medicine with prayer is a crucial step in the healing process.

In this country, all medicine is anointed by the Food and Drug Administration, whose seal of approval is given to those compounds that pass inspection. But sanctifying the medicine itself and honoring the sacred nature of the healing process might be, I was coming to believe, just as important.

The Medicine Buddha practice can be used to bless medicines of all types—common household pills, liniments, herbs, or prescription medicines. Though the ritual is best performed by a lama, it can be performed as a blessing by anyone who has sincere belief in the healing power of Medicine Buddha.

Much later, the Venerable Tenzin Gephel, a senior teacher at Namgyal, explained during a lecture that the most important aspect of a mantra is the motivation behind its repetition. Repeating a mantra for personal benefit, he said, is not very different than behaving like an animal. Animals know how to care for themselves but cannot extend that care to others. The only truly enlightened motivation is the determination to help others.[5]

Many in the Tibetan community believe that given this special spiritual attention, all medicines gain in potency. Others say that Tibetan medicine is fully effective without any spiritual intervention. Personally, I am convinced that the selfless intentions and magnificent vision surrounding the ancient practice of Medicine Buddha can only be of benefit in the struggle against illness in all of its manifestations.

Blessing the Medicine

Here is a shortened form of the blessing we were taught:

In a clean space, cover a small table with a cloth and sprinkle some rice on it as an offering. Then, place the medicine (or imagine it) in a precious bowl of some type.

Imagine before you the Medicine Buddha, surrounded by enlightened beings. Acknowledge your profound respect for the Three Jewels and your reliance on their help.

Make a sincere request for healing from the many diseases which originate from the three poisons of anger, attachment, and ignorance.

Now recite the Medicine Buddha mantra: "Tayata Om Bekhanze Bekhanze Maha Bekhanze Bekhanze Radza Samungate Soha."

As you recite the mantra, imagine brilliant lights emanating from the heart centers of Medicine Buddha and the other enlightened beings. Visualize that these lights are absorbed by the medicine and acknowledge that they impart to it enhanced ability to alleviate suffering, disease, and illness.

Finally, envision the assembly of enlightened beings dissolving into the medicine. Put a small portion of the medicine on your tongue, and taste it as a blessing.

CHAPTER THREE

The Teachings of Medicine Buddha

While Khensur Rinpoche and the monks guided participants at the Ithaca retreat in the spiritual aspects of Medicine Buddha, medical doctors explained the practical teachings of Tibetan healing. Together (they actually sat side by side for much of the week), Dr. Tenzin Dakpa, who spoke excellent English, and Dr. D. Dawa worked their way through the key features of Tibetan healing practice—no easy task, as it turned out.

Although Dr. Dakpa was both mild mannered and soft spoken, he was no stranger to the lecture circuit. By the time he reached Ithaca, he had presented Tibetan medical ideas and offered consultations in eight European countries. He had also served as resident Tibetan doctor in Tibetan medical clinics in Pokhara, Nepal, and New Delhi, India.

Dr. Dawa held the position of Deputy Director of the Materia Medica Department of Men Tsee Khang. His educational background included not only medicine, but also Chinese literature and painting. A writer, artist, and top scholar, he, too, had lectured and consulted widely, largely in Europe and Japan.

In a series of ten lectures, each an hour-and-a-half long, Dr. Dawa, the senior physician, and Dr. Dakpa, who helped translate, presented a detailed explanation of the physical aspects of Tibetan medicine.

BALANCE AND THE FIVE ELEMENTS

Five elements form the foundation of the universe and are primary constituents of living bodies. From earth, the bones, flesh, and the sense of smell are formed. From water, blood, other body fluids, and the sense of taste are created. Fire brings heat, digestion, and the ability to see. Air is responsible for respiration and the sense of touch. Space allows for room between the organs and tissues and brings the sense of hearing. The birth of the elements is commemorated in this thangka displayed by Men Tsee Khang.

As is the case in many Eastern healing systems, the concept of balance is fundamental to Tibetan healing practices. Essentially, good health requires that the microcosm of the body be in accord with the macrocosm of the universe. This balance is achieved by the quality of the relationship among the five universal elements—earth, water, fire, air, and space. Ultimately, these elements make up both the human body and external world.

So basic are these elements to human life in the Tibetan system that it is thought that when the elements of the body cease functioning, death occurs. *The Tibetan Book of the Dead* describes the actual process of dying in detail. As we die, the elements which constitute the body disintegrate, returning one by one to their original states. First, earth dissolves into water; then water sinks into fire, fire into air, and air into space. External and internal signs signal each stage of the process. As the elements dissipate, our senses fail and, according to the kind of life we have led, we lapse into the various states of consciousness that arise in the interval between this life and the next. Experienced meditators are taught to recognize these signs so as to mediate their own dying process toward a favorable rebirth.

The discussion about the nature of the elements has never been restricted to Tibet. The Rishis of old India meditated on the topic, and their conclusions were used to form the basis of Ayurvedic medicine. The Chinese sages and Greek philosophers did the same. The medical systems of all of these countries

clearly reflect the notion that at the heart of existence lie certain basic elements.

The debate has been ongoing for millennia. In the middle of the third century BC, for example, Aristotle challenged Platonic philosophers about the nature of the elements and how they came into being. In arguing his case, Aristotle had this to say: "For in the whole range of time past, so far as our inherited records reach, no change appears to have taken place either in the whole scheme of the outermost heavens or in any of its proper parts. . . . And so, implying that the primary body is something else beyond earth, fire, air and water, they gave the highest place a name of its own, *aither*, derived from the fact that it 'runs always' for an eternity of time."[6]

The Tibetan system of correspondences between the five elements and other aspects of life is elaborate and multifaceted. The elements are linked with astrological phenomena, the seasons, the directions, physical matter, and everything else that falls within the field of human consciousness. In the centuries of debate and discussion over this issue, it has generally been decided that the qualities of the elements enable relationships among living tissues.

On another level, the qualities of elements also provide a convenient metaphor to describe various processes. Earth, for example, is stable and solid and thus provides a foundation. Water enables cohesion. Fire helps things to mature and ripen. Air makes growth possible. Space ensures room for movement.

By investigating these cosmic constants, the Tibetan physician is able to help patients harmonize with the natural order of things. Tibetan medicines themselves are created from planetary counterparts of the five elements, which are found throughout the natural world—in plants, minerals, waters, precious gems, even in animals. In this way, a bridge is built, reconnecting the basic constituents in the individual to the rest of creation.

The essence of Tibetan healing, which might take a doctor ten or more years to learn, is diagnosing exactly which elements are lacking or in excess in a patient's body and prescribing the right compound to restore the system to balance. If a patient, for example, is diagnosed as having an inflammation of the stomach and intestines, a medicine with cooling properties may be prescribed.

One of the ingredients might be the seeds of the *Herpetospermum pendunculosum*, a member of the gourd or cucumber family. This plant is known to have cooling properties which would counteract the excessive heat generated by an inflammation. The plant is also understood to have a bitter taste.

Taste is important, because, from it, it is possible to derive the elemental composition of a particular substance. In the case of the seeds of the gourd, the bitter taste is known to be comprised of the two elements water and air. Each of these elements has its own distinct healing properties. Medicines made with the water element, for example, have both a cooling quality and a unifying effect in the body. Medicines made from the air element tend to cool as well, but they also lighten, roughen, dry, absorb, and increase mobility.

THE THREE HUMORS

The idea of balance is developed further in Tibetan healing by the theory of humors. In this context, *humor* refers to three physical substances which lead to three specific "temperaments" or "habitual dispositions." It also conveys information about a person's physical or body type. Categorizing people according to their humors facilitates the process of initial diagnosis and guides medical practitioners in prescribing appropriate treatments.

The Tibetans are not the only people to make the theory of humors central to their healing system. The Greeks, Persians, and Indians were

also familiar with this concept, which was common throughout the ancient world. Even as late as Shakespeare's time, Western medicine was partly based on a system of humors. Hamlet, for instance, is described as "melancholic," one of four medieval humors—sanguine, choleric, melancholic, phlegmatic—thought to categorize all humankind.

The modern Tibetan system of humors owes a great deal—indeed much of its medical theory in general—to Ayurveda, the traditional healing system of India. The Ayurvedic system classifies ideas about individuals, diseases, and cures according to the predominance of one of three bodily humors. Essentially, each person is thought to contain a particular, though typically unequal, balance among these three. Exactly how the humors are combined in any individual will determine, in part, his or her disposition, physiological type, and so on. When the humors are working as they should, they are said to be in balance. When they are out of kilter, a doctor or a lama may need to intervene.

In Ayurveda, the humors are called *Vatta, Pitta,* and *Kapha* and have many associations, including a means to classify body and personality types. Classification of body types is also well known to Western science, where they have been described as endomorphic (inner), mesomorphic (middle), and ectomorphic (outer). Tibetan physicians know these humors as *lung, tripa,* and *beygen.* These terms are usually translated into English as "wind," "bile," and "phlegm," but each term is much more complex than the simple English translations would indicate. Each humor, for instance, is further classified into five categories, making fifteen major subdivisions in all. These categories enable the physician

VATTA   PITTA   KAPHA

The three humors, Vatta, Pitta, Kapha, as they influence body types in Ayurveda.

to arrive at sophisticated assessments of a patient's condition.

Tibetan physicians believe that the humors do not operate exclusively in the physical body, but also in the subtle body, its invisible counterpart. The theory is that the subtle body is comprised of vibrations, energy currents, and energy centers, which, although largely undetectable without special training, are nevertheless very real. These subtle forces are also influenced by the disposition of the humors.

The Three Humors

The first humor, *lung* or wind, is associated with the air element and is one of the principal energies in the body. Historically and even today, it has been associated with the breathing process and with breath itself. More than this, in one of its aspects, wind is considered to be an energy or principle of movement coupled with the breath itself. Often referred to as "the life force," it is responsible for many functions such as breathing, movement, birth, blood circulation, and mental operations. The texts often refer to it as the "carrier of consciousness." Wind has a number of defining characteristics such as coarse, light, cold, subtle, hard, and motile.

The second humor, *tripa* or bile, is associated with the fire element. Its nature is said to be hot, oily, sharp, malodorous, purging, and moist. This energy helps us digest food and drink, clears the complexion, provides heat for the body and blood, and brings clarity to the senses and to the mind.

The third humor, *beygen* or phlegm, is associated with the earth and water elements. It is considered a cooling energy. Its character-

istics are oily, cool, heavy, blunt, smooth, firm, and sticky. Its energy helps us in the stretching and protection of limbs, in regulating the fluids in the body, in calming the body, and in sleeping well.

As one might expect, the humors are formed from various combinations of the five elements. For each of us, the elements which combine to make up our body/mind are constituted in a particular way according to our karmic predisposition. It is no accident that we find ourselves in our particular worldly circumstance. Simply put, our "very subtle mind"—the essence or thread that links together our various lives—driven by karma, is irresistibly attracted to appropriate parents.

In short, we create our own destiny. Our own actions determine our fate, including the genetic inheritance we receive from our parents. Our life circumstances, then, are of our own making. In my own case, this was a highly intimidating thought.

THE DISTANT CAUSES OF DISEASE

We were now well into the retreat. Although I had heard quite a number of fantastic theories, the implications of this grand theory were overwhelming. In my mind's eye, a giant cosmic finger seemed to point directly at me. The unvoiced accusation was quite clear: Only I was responsible for my life situation—my relationships, my health, my finances, even my likes and dislikes. Further, the only means of improving my fate was improving myself. Given that I had a lifetime of comfortable habits to overcome, I knew full well that improvement of this sort could only mean a great deal of work.

I found my mind wandering to other beliefs about destiny. I reflected for a time on the virtues of ancient Greek cosmology, in which a

whimsical god or goddess could be blamed completely for one's fate. These great beings could also, according to mythology, be persuaded and even bribed into relenting. Unfortunately, it was perfectly evident that such was not at all the case in the Tibetan belief system.

I was also bothered by the confusing question of the humors and how they are able to organize the primal elements into an appropriate body. Exactly what is it that informs the humors? Once again, the Tibetans doctors presented an ingenious explanation. The three mind poisons themselves inform, indeed, actually create the humors: ignorance (or close-mindedness) is the source of phlegm; desire, of wind; and aversion (or hatred), of bile. Since the poisons work at this root level, they are classified as the distant causes of disease.

Essentially, then, our bodies form according to our psychological dispositions. Even after death, it seems, we are not free of ourselves, since our basic predisposition—our essence as molded by the poisons—lingers in the in-between state, informing our experience there and propelling us to our next incarnation.

Now, unless you have entertained the possibility of reincarnation, this order of things might never be considered, for it would seem to be a case of placing the cart before the horse. In the West we usually assume that our psychology is the product of our education and upbringing—not something we ourselves created the causes for before our current life.

After having thoroughly explained the relationship between the poisons and the humors, Dr. Dakpa told us that, unfortunately, there was little any of us could do to influence the mind poisons directly. Influence at this level might be accomplished by a high lama possessing great mental and spiritual powers but definitely not by everyday people. The rest of us had to rely on ordinary doctors such as himself. For some reason—perhaps it was relief—this remark struck us as hilarious, because everyone present broke into gales of laughter.

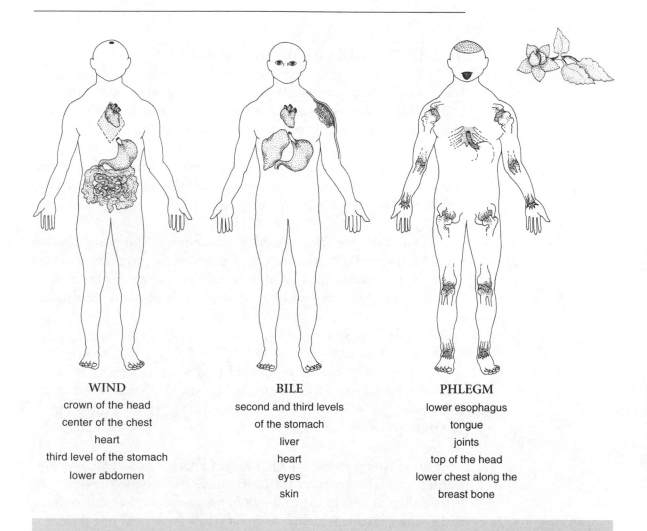

WIND	BILE	PHLEGM
crown of the head	second and third levels	lower esophagus
center of the chest	of the stomach	tongue
heart	liver	joints
third level of the stomach	heart	top of the head
lower abdomen	eyes	lower chest along the
	skin	breast bone

The three humors originate in the mental realm as a direct result of the actions of the three mind poisons. In the physical realm, their first action is to organize the five primal elements into living beings. These beings, human, animal, or otherwise, reflect patterns of thought and behavior exhibited in past lives. The humors will continue to influence the general predisposition of these beings, including such characteristics as illness, attitude, and preferences, for the duration of their lives. Each humor has many functions and is related to many different operations of the body. This illustration describes their general locations.

THE PROXIMATE CAUSES OF DISEASE

When the laughter subsided, Dr. Dakpa began again by introducing an entirely different category of causes for disease, which he termed "proximate causes." For a Westerner, these were easier to understand, because at least three of the causes corresponded to beliefs common to Western medicine. In this class, Dr. Dakpa outlined four general categories: the effects of seasonal change, unwholesome diet, inappropriate behavior, and actions from past lives.

Putting aside for the moment my discomfort with past lives as a cause for disease, I concentrated my attention on the three causes I could accept without question. The intimate relationship among the time of year, the foods I ate, my activities, and my health was quite clear to me.

Seasonal Changes

A writer's life unavoidably includes weeks and even years of extremely sedentary activity, sitting at a desk and writing. At these times, it becomes unwise for me to eat certain foods—ice cream, for example, or drink fermented beverages.

Further, the seasons play a large role in both my diet and behavior. Winters in Idaho are quite long. My horse and I both know that an extra dollop of oats in the cold weather is important to heat the body and fend off disease. The simple fact is that a large bowl of porridge is the only winter breakfast that keeps me warm and full until lunch. In summer, however, I never willingly eat the stuff.

Seasonal change has long been known to play a major role in physiological change. It is no accident that bears hibernate, birds migrate, and flowers bloom when they do. Everything that lives responds to seasonal change. The length of day, the intensity of sunlight, the daily temperature, the amount of available moisture all induce specific responses from living beings.

If you doubt that our physical bodies change with the seasons, consider the seasonal transformation of animals. In fall, a black bear's coat is thick and sleek, the result of a summer's foraging. The colors of the brook trout become almost iridescent when they spawn in the fall. Every winter, the fur of the snowshoe hare changes color to match the snow perfectly.

Careful observation of the seasons allows us to note changes in ourselves as well. According to the seasons, we can determine when to reduce our intake of certain foods and what to introduce in their place. And, as the doctors were careful to point out, eating the wrong foods can actually damage our bodies.

Disregarding seasonal dietary requirements can easily lead to the accumulation of excessive amounts of one or more humors. The resulting imbalance can result in sickness. During the heat of mid-summer, eating too many hot foods, such as peppers, many grains, nuts, or oily foods, will, sooner or later, lead to bile diseases.

An excessive accumulation of bile in the body during the summer, for example, can appear as a bile disease in the fall. By winter, the bile begins to disperse and, correspondingly, the disease begins to subside. Of interest, the same excess of bile which causes disease during hot weather may prevent it in a cold season.

At any rate, like the other humors, a bile disease can manifest in many seemingly unrelated parts of the body. Some of the more important areas include the digestion, body heat, clarity of vision, the coloration of blood and skin, general vigor of the body and, surprisingly, our conduct. Poor functioning in any of these general categories suggests an imbalance—either a deficiency or an excess—in the bile humor.

Food

In large measure, it is the cook who determines the health of the

family. There is much truth in the old story about the country doctor who, before examining his patients, made a habit of inspecting their kitchens. The doctor knew that if we select and prepare our foods carefully, they will work much like medicine, not only nourishing but also healing us. He is also aware that negligence in the kitchen can certainly cause illness.

In Tibetan healing, it is generally understood that chronic internal illnesses often begin with what appears to be a simple case of indigestion. As we know from Western science, food is broken down during the digestive process into its basic elements. These are stored as packets of energy to be assimilated later into the body. If this process is not working properly, disease can easily take hold.

A weak digestive process may not produce enough digestive fire, the heat required to break down food. As a consequence, the body's processing system cannot extract nutrition from food efficiently. On the other hand, an improperly functioning digestive system can produce too much fire, a condition which can result in abnormally high blood temperatures.

The importance of determining the most suitable diet for ourselves according to the season is obvious. But to do this properly, we must not only thoroughly understand our own constitution but study the relationship between various foods and the five elements. Interestingly, Tibetans regard taste to be the primary means through which we can evaluate the foods we need. According to the theory, when the five elements combine in foods, they produce the variety of taste sensations we experience when we eat.

Many sweet-tasting foods, for example, are generated from earth and water. Sweet foods include white sugar, grains, and vegetables. These foods often, though not always, have a cooling effect. White sugar, for example, is very cooling and only advisable for those with a predominance of bile. Brown sugar and molasses, on the other hand, while sweet

in taste, have more of a more warming quality.

The table below describes the general relationship among food types and their tastes, and elemental composition. Learning about the qualities of foods enables us to make healthful decisions about what we eat, how we cook, and even when we dine. As a result, we begin to understand ourselves in new ways and see the consequences of our diets.

For instance, a passion for sweets and raw vegetables may lead to digestive problems. When taken in excess, sweets and raw vegetables can extinguish the digestive fire, a term describing the chemical reactions common to normal digestion. The fire is produced by the bile in the digestive system. As a consequence, phlegm increases to dangerous levels. The end result is a progressive attrition of the digestive process. Very gradually, both the kidney and the liver lose strength.

The Elemental Composition of Foods

Taste	Composition	Food Types
Sweet	water and earth	fruits, grains, milk
Sour	earth and fire	some fruits, fermented foods
Salty	fire and water	seaweed, watery vegetables
Bitter	water and wind	lettuce, spinach, endives, celery
Pungent	fire and wind	peppers, garlic, ginger
Astringent	earth and wind	legumes, mushrooms

Behavior

Tibetan healing theory regards behavior as anything you might say, do, feel, or think. In fact, everything we do affects the balance of humors. Sleeping, working, exercising, eating, discussing, writing, complaining, and so on, all can produce an imbalance. Nothing is exempt.

The concept of excess and deficiency helps us determine what is and what is not a balanced action. For our purposes, it is essential to understand that 1) excessive or deficient behavior in one or more activities can ruin health; 2) sound health requires a balance among the activities of everyday life; and 3) what is normal or sensible for one individual may be excessive or deficient for another.

Another way to look at behavior is whether or not it is out of the ordinary. Modern psychiatry has a vast terminology which describes unusual behavior: neurosis, obsession, compulsion, to name three types. Since these afflictions are well known, it is not necessary to describe them in detail here. But it is interesting to note that these terms connect behaviors to states of mind. In other words, mental actions, what we call states of mind, are regarded as the source of physical and verbal habits. Of course, Buddhist teachings say the same thing.

Yet another distinction is between irregular and habitual behavior. In terms of health, irregular behavior is not so great a concern as is habitual behavior. A night or two with little sleep, or a few days of long hours at the office, for instance, are probably nothing to worry about. As any insomniac or workaholic will tell you, however, regular sleep deprivation or a compulsion to work incessantly often lead to major health problems.

What is of particular interest to the Tibetan physician is how the repetition associated with habits leads to excessive buildup of one or more humors. The end result of an excess in one or more of the humors is inevitably some mental or physical disturbance. At one point during

a lecture on habitual behavior, Dr. Dawa illustrated the connection with a joke. You Westerners are so busy, he said with a smile, you do not even have time to use the bathroom. This habit, he added to everyone's amusement, has an unfortunate consequence. It causes constipation.

A very broad yet distinct category of actions is those known as "temporary" behaviors. These include the involuntary or necessary activities of our bodies, such as sleeping, eating, drinking, yawning, breathing, urination, and so on. Under normal conditions, none of these activities should ever be suppressed, since doing so leads to special problems. Preventing yourself from sneezing, for example, can lead to a diminishing of the senses, while refusing to sleep brings on sluggishness and poor digestive processes.

The relationship between our behavior and the humors is clearly delineated, and each of the humors is itself related to a specific set of problems. Mental behavior is often cited in relation to wind. Excessive thinking, for example, can lead to wind disturbances. Other factors leading to wind disturbances are long periods of sorrow or crying, compulsive talking, eating foods low in nutrition, loss of blood, strenuous activity when one is hungry, sleeplessness, irregular meals, and prolonged exposure to drafts and cold. Frequent yawning, trembling, extreme hunger, lightheadedness, pains which seem to shift about the body, twitching, restlessness, and psychological imbalances are some prominent symptoms of a wind disorder.

Bile disorders are often caused by excessive physical labor or exercise, especially when it takes place in the sun or near a source of heat. Too much alcohol, meat, or foods that are sharp, hot, and oily can have the same effect, especially on those who are consistently engaged in heavy physical work. Some symptoms of bile disorders include nausea, headaches, a bitter taste in the mouth, great heat in the body, and pains in the upper back and body.

Behavior also affects the third humor, phlegm. Immersion in cold

water or residing in damp and cold climates unfavorably affects this humor, as does excessive eating. As Dr. Dawa expressed it, scrunching up his face as he did so, "these people cannot stop eating. They are always eating, eating, eating." Foods that are cool, sticky, heavy, and stored for long periods in tins can increase phlegm. Symptoms of a phlegm disorder include indigestion, little appetite, inability to taste, internal and external chills, belching, and regurgitation.

Since poor eating habits are a major cause of humoral disturbances, traditional Tibetan healing has a simple rule of thumb. The theory maintains that each of us has a different sized stomach. So, there are corresponding limits to what we can ingest and remain healthy. To discover these limits, we imagine the stomach as having four quadrants. After eating, two of these sections should be filled with solid food, one with liquid, and one should be kept empty. Diligently eating in this way will do much to ensure our health. Unfortunately, doing so requires considerable self-restraint.

Aging

Our behavior must also be adjusted to suit our age. The simple fact is that the older we are, the less strength we have. We simply are not capable of the same exertions as in our youth. Nevertheless, we often try to force our bodies to behave as they did in younger days. Persisting in this belief, of course, can only lead to injury.

Another consequence of aging is that the action of the humors begins to change. Tibetan medical texts state that in childhood, phlegm predominates. In middle age, bile is the prevalent humor; while in old age, wind rules the body. As a result, wind disorders, for example, are more difficult to cure in elderly people than in other

Dr. Dawa, Tibetan physican and scholar, has lectured and consulted extensively in Europe and Japan.

age groups. As you might expect, phlegm disorders are most difficult to treat in childhood, and bile disorders in middle age.

If you study the characteristics of elderly people, it is not difficult to see the symptoms of an excess of wind. Frequent sighing, yawning, and stretching the limbs are all symptoms of an excess of wind. Elderly people also have a tendency toward lightheadedness, and their thoughts wander. They experience ringing sounds in their ears, and their vision declines. They tend to sleep poorly, find their mouths and throats dry, and experience pains which seem to shift about in the body, particularly in the hip and joints.

ACTIONS FROM PAST LIVES

It was not at all difficult for me to understand how the seasons, diet, behavior, and aging could bring about illness. Full acceptance of the possibility that actions from past lives could influence our state of health, however, still eluded me. After hearing about the relationship between the mind poisons and the humors, I came away from the retreat with some conception of how such a connection might be possible. Some-time later, I pieced together an outline of what the doctors had been saying.

I came to understand that if past lives were to have influences, these impulses must be very deeply seated indeed, well below the threshold of consciousness. I also realized that these influences would have to be so subtle that they would go virtually unnoticed to all but the most highly trained minds. Years before, I had studied hypnosis and had seen the deeper layers of the mind revealed firsthand. I had no doubt that these deeper layers did indeed exert a profound influence in our every-day lives.

At one point, during a session on age regression, a member of the class blurted out a question: "Have you ever brought a person back to a

time before their birth?" The instructor's reply was both tactful and compelling. "That is one question I choose not to answer."

Typically, educators and psychologists in the West explain behavior in terms of genetics and environment. Genetic predisposition is usually thought to be responsible for the great majority of our behavior. The remainder is felt to be due to our environmental conditioning.

Over the years, I had adopted these notions without even questioning them. I understood the nature/nurture discussion, as it is called, to be the only possible way to explain our actions. Now, after the lectures by the Tibetans, I had another powerful tool. Personally, I have never succeeded in lifting the veil of either the past or the future. So I have no direct means to verify the notion of past-life influences. Nevertheless, the idea is certainly worth keeping in mind. Perhaps one day, through the action of the medicine of the dharma, my horizons will broaden a little more.

Dr. Dakpa lectures on Tibetan medicine and utilizes a medical thangka to make a point.

NEXT STEPS

By the time Drs. Dawa and Dakpa had finished their presentations, I was certain of two things. First, I wanted to learn more. The Tibetan system of healing struck me as empowering and full of grace. It was clear that here was a system with real potential to help its adherents lead a long and healthy life.

Second, I wanted to move beyond theory and see this healing sys-

tem in action. I decided to sign up for a medical appointment with a traditional Tibetan doctor. Little did I suspect that as a result of this interview, I would travel to a country where Tibetan medicine is not considered a strange and antiquated mystical practice but is the highly esteemed medicine of an ancient and venerable culture.

Journey to Bodhnath

The quickest way to find out how Tibetan medical ideas are applied is to be examined by a Tibetan doctor. So, overcoming my long-standing fear of medical people of any persuasion, I made an appointment for a consultation with Dr. Dawa.

Not everything a Tibetan doctor does is foreign to the Western way of thinking. The first thing I had to do, for example, was sign a release form. That was easy. The instructions themselves, though, were somewhat more difficult to comprehend. They read, in part:

"Dear Peter: You will need to bring with you a sample of your first morning urine and complete the form that is enclosed. Bringing former medical reports is optional. The physician will examine the urine as well as feel your pulse in several spots and may inquire into your medical history."

I am not squeamish, but I confess to a certain reluctance when it comes to urinanalysis. Nevertheless, in the interests of medical science, I dutifully filled my bottle, closed it with a tightly fitting lid, and walked slowly and carefully to the appointment location.

After the preliminary greetings, Dr. Dawa examined the contents of my bottle with care, checking its color, vapor, smell, and bubbles. Urine characteristic of a wind disorder is bluish and has big bubbles. If it is

reddish-yellow with thick sediments and a foul smell, there is a problem with the bile. If it is white, has few sediments, and is without smell, the condition is identified with phlegm. As it turns out, my sample was quite normal. My examiner knew this immediately. Healthy urine, it seems, is whitish-yellow and smells like sheep dung.

Putting the bottle down, Dr. Dawa placed the first three fingers of his right hand on my left wrist and "listened." In Tibetan practice, pulse taking is not a straightforward matter. Historically, pulse reading was conducted with the patient at rest, at dawn. "When the sun rises in the east," the text reads, "but before the rays have touched the ground, is the time to read the pulse." The meaning is clear: to read a pulse, a doctor requires light to see and the patient to be at rest. There is also a more subtle explanation: the period before sunrise is the best time for meditation and concentration. It is also a transition period for the patient, between sleeping and waking, between rest and activity.

Dr. Dawa then reversed hands, using his left to read the pulse on my right wrist. Only three fingers on each hand are used to read the various pulses (yes, Tibetan doctors recognize many kinds of pulses), but each finger is considered to have two halves, making twelve sections in all. Each section is associated with an organ and an element, giving the doctor a view of the internal landscape of the patient.

In part, the doctor uses the span of time between his own inhalations and exhalations to determine the health of the patient's pulse. If it is healthy, it will beat five times in this span of time. A regular pulse throughout the reading is considered a sign of health. Otherwise, there is a problem. Faster or slower rates indicate hot or cold disorders respectively, and the specific frequency suggests how serious an illness it is.

After what seemed an eternity, the doctor smiled a knowing smile and asked to look at my tongue. "I have found a heart disorder," he announced a moment later.

Why I laughed, I'm not certain. During a previous lecture, he had explained about the tongue. "The tongue of someone with a wind disorder will be red, covered with small pimples, and have a dry and coarse texture. The tongue has a close relation to the heart. Someone who has a heart disorder caused by 'wind' will have a crack in the center of their tongue." After that lecture, I had studied my tongue in the mirror and suspected the worst. Now my suspicions had been confirmed.

"You have too much heat," said Dr. Dawa. "You have to bring this condition into balance. Be very careful about your diet. What sort of things are you eating now?"

I told him about the oatmeal and toast and about the eggs and pancakes. No meat, I said, but when I mentioned chicken and fish, he interjected. "Fish and chicken are good for you but not red meat. Cut back on chicken in summer. It produces too much heat. What do you drink?"

I had purposely avoided telling him about the coffee and beer, but he left me no choice. "I have the occasional beer," I mumbled. Then, with a sinking feeling, I confessed to the coffee. "And I drink quite a bit of coffee. I also drink plenty of water," I added, hoping in some way for absolution.

No such luck. The doctor began, "Stay away from alcohol. And from coffee, too. It is bitter and produces heat. And do not eat dairy products. Do you know about Vegan diets?"

"Yes," I said, the sinking feeling returning. I had heard of them. Never having had a great deal of self-discipline, I knew that it would be highly unlikely for me to stick with any kind of diet, let alone one as strict as Vegan, which is completely vegetarian with no dairy products or eggs.

He concluded by asking about my work habits. I told him about our country life—shoveling the snow from the roofs, splitting and stacking firewood, building our house. Then I talked about my writing and

how I could become preoccupied with it, even to the point of obsession.

Dr. Dawa's concluding statement surprised me. "Too much physical work is bad for your heart. Too much mental work makes you light-headed. You must bring these two work habits into balance."

After an interview and examination which lasted about forty-five minutes, Dr. Dawa wrote a traditional prescription. The doctor had convinced me that, given a chance, his medicine could help. He also convinced me that I had to know more.

Then he wrote out a prescription. "Try this," he said, "and see if it helps. You have nothing to lose." He explained that he couldn't fill the prescription until he returned to his office in India in six or eight weeks. Then there would be mail delivery time; India was a long way from here. But I was not to worry; the medication would arrive in due time.

"Yes," I remember thinking, "India is a long way from here." I had no idea at the time, of course, that I would discover soon enough exactly how far it is.

MY PILGRIMAGE BEGINS

Always eager to learn, especially when learning is accompanied by adventure, I decided to travel to Asia to see how Tibetan healing is practiced. I hoped to interview Tibetan healers and their patients and to observe traditional healing in action.

Two years later, on a mild March afternoon, I landed in Katmandu, Nepal, surely one of the strangest cities on the planet. At one time, Katmandu was considered a sacred place, rivaling any in the world. But at the close of the twentieth century, it was apparent that much had changed.

Still, the place was ablaze with color and with a seemingly infinite variety and intensity of sounds, sights, and smells. I was overwhelmed.

Fortunately, my assignment lent me the support and the direction I needed to get grounded. I had come to discover as much as I could about the healing practices of the Himalayas, particularly Tibetan healing. The texts I had read and the lectures I had heard had provided the theory, but only in Asia could I investigate these traditions firsthand.

Prior to my departure, I had ferreted out a few names and addresses of likely contacts. This effort, I hoped, would get me started and save me some footwork. As it turned out, however, my preparation was only a little help. Most of my most significant encounters happened through coincidence and good luck. On the spot introductions were also helpful and, when all else failed, bribery—*baksheesh*, as it is called—worked quite nicely, too.

A few kilometers from Katmandu, on its eastern side, is the town of Bodhnath. Since it is situated on several major trade routes, including one with Lhasa, Tibet, Bodhnath has always been a convenient gateway to the neighboring metropolis. As a result, it is populated by traders, particularly Tibetans who excel in this business. This is as true today as it has been in the past. So, with its large Tibetan population and high concentration of monasteries, Bodhnath seemed like the place to begin. I booked a room at the Rabsel, reputed to be the best guesthouse in town. Fortunately these reports proved to be correct, and its quiet quarters provided a welcome sanctuary at the end of each day.

The Plight of the Poor

Anyone contemplating a trip to Katmandu be forewarned. This is not a destination for the faint-hearted. Before I left Idaho, someone had predicted that my trip would be an assault on the senses. The characterization was accurate in the extreme. From the moment I left the airport

until I returned two months later, a seemingly infinite array of smells, sounds, and colors wrestled daily for my attention. Coming from an empty, silent, cold place, usually odorless, and colored only by the whites, grays, and greens of winter in the coniferous forest, I found this teeming city to be otherworldly. The clamorous ravings of shopkeepers and rickshaw drivers, the continual bickering with street vendors, and the constant honking of horns composed an aural soundscape that was impossible to tune out.

Disease, poverty, pollution, overcrowding, and corruption were everywhere. I was swimming in a vast sea of human beings, most of whom seemed to be vying for what little money I possessed. I found this most difficult when I passed beggars, orphans, lepers, the homeless, the sick, and the disabled, knowing that for these unfortunates, begging had become a business. Day after day, bright and early, I watched this ragtag army filter into position along well-known tourist routes. After exchanging courtesies with their neighbors, they got down to business. Without mercy, they accosted tourist after tourist or anyone at all who might have a spare rupee. Never once, though, did I see them pester a lama, and never once did I see a lama offer alms.

Visiting every agency trying to alleviate suffering in Nepal would be an impossible task. By one estimate, as many as 25,000 non-governmental organizations (NGOs) are currently working to provide relief and other forms of aid in the Katmandu Valley alone. This staggering number suggests the magnitude of the problems in this region.

It took many days of exposure to the poverty-stricken chaos of the street before I could relax, even a little. Once I did, I knew without doubt that I had come to the right place. If the spirit of traditional healing were alive, here was its testing ground. But could any kind of healing, I wondered, address this confusion of human misery?

It was obvious that in this part of the world,

medical attention is not widely available. Medical people of any description are few in number, and medical treatment is, as I discovered, not free. I spent many hours in Tibetan clinics and other small medical centers making appointments, conducting interviews, observing clients, and talking to staff. Since I was primarily interested in the impact of Tibetan healing on the lives of ordinary people, I restricted my investigations to smaller operations which served the local community.

Inside a Tibetan Medical Clinic

While in Bodhnath, I visited three Tibetan medical clinics. This turned out to be no easy feat because knowing that a place exists in Katmandu and actually finding it are not the same thing. Maps are essentially useless, since none exist with reliable detail. I spent unusually long periods standing on the street, pouring over what maps there are, in a hopeless attempt to determine my whereabouts. This proved to be a very frustrating exercise, since nothing much was accomplished, except that a large crowd invariably gathered around me in a vain attempt to help. The best way to get around is to take a motorized rickshaw to the nearest neighborhood and then ask. This method, unlike map reading, generally works.

One of the three clinics I visited, in the nearby village of Chabahil, was associated with Men Tsee Khang. The other two, the Kunphen Clinic in Chhetrapati and the Traditional Tibetan Clinic in Bodhnath, are run by Tibetan doctors in private practice. Doctors who work privately forego the sponsorship of Men Tsee Khang and the supply of medicine which is difficult to produce independently.

While there must be other ramifications of this autonomy, one obvious one is the source of the medicines dispensed. Dr. Kunsang Dorjee of the Kunphen Clinic told me that he buys Tibetan medicine directly from Tibet, now, of course, under the control of the Chinese, and not from Men Tsee Khang in Dharamsala, where medicine is also made.

Although there seems to be some rivalry between the independents and Men Tsee Khang, the Kunphen Clinic has been in business for twenty years, and it is apparent that its independent status has not in any way harmed its business interests. In fact, on both of my visits to this clinic, it was packed. For an hour or more, upwards of thirty clients sat outside in the open air on wooden benches, patiently waiting their turns. Much to their amusement, I sat with them, making small talk and inquiring as unobtrusively as possible into their health and the purpose for their visit.

This sign welcomes visitors to the Kunphen Clinic in Chhetrapati. Though fading in places, it clearly informs clients of its unusual services. Where else might a client find Wish Fulfilling Pills?

I had not intended to seek a medical consultation during this visit but simply to meet the doctor, wander about and observe, ask questions of the staff whenever possible, and glean a general sense of how the clinic worked.

Eventually, my name was called, and I took my place inside the building. Here, too, several patients waited. We sat quietly watching a Tibetan pharmacist filling prescriptions. Behind her, medical compounds that had been rolled and pressed into perfectly round balls were stored in large glass bottles lining the walls. There were dozens of these containers. After reading each prescription, she carefully labeled a small brown paper bag and then filled it with pills, or *rilbu*, from the appropriate bottles.

A single rilbu, I later discovered, can contain 170 or more ingredients. Each ingredient is carefully prepared and measured. Some accounts say that the Tibetan pharmacopoeia is larger than that of traditional Chinese medicine and that more than a thousand preparations can be made.

The body of knowledge about preparing and administering remedies is known in Tibetan healing as the "medicine of substances." Substances used in medicines are organized into three basic groups which correspond to the three kingdoms: animal, vegetable, and mineral. However, since Buddhism is adverse to taking any life, the use of animal products has declined in recent years. Further, many animals used in the past, such as the black rhinoceros, the wolf, the tiger and the wild yak are now quite rare, even close to extinction, and difficult to obtain. Historically, though, animal products played an important role in Tibetan medicine. The use of minerals and precious substances in medications is still common, but here, too, their use has declined, since many traditional ingredients such as gold, diamond and sapphire are now very expensive. For these reasons, there is little doubt that the emphasis in Tibetan medications will continue its shift toward plants.

In recent years, another significant change has taken place. It is well known that mountain environments are very sensitive and that even slight intrusions can have disastrous ecological consequences. Until recently, expeditions by doctors and other herb gatherers in search of healing plants have not seemed to have a significant impact. However, with the current worldwide interest in Tibetan medicine, the demand for these plants is increasing at an alarming rate.

The Mandala of the Sun is a rilbu with only ten ingredients, including cinnamon, long pepper, cardamom, asparagus, and honey. It works as a tonic for the kidneys and bladder and is effective against cold disorders, such as arthritis and diarrhea. A typical dosage would be two or three grams every day, taken with warm water.

As well, more Tibetan doctors are graduating from institutions in India and Tibet each year. If the main source of ingredients for their medications continues to be wild plants, disaster for the Himalayan ecosystem can be the only consequence. The devastation of the wild orchid population in the Indian forests at the hands of the orchid sellers is clear

Animal Parts Traditionally Used in Tibetan Medicine

ANIMAL	PART
Ass	testes
Bear	gall
Deer	horn
Dragon	bones
Elephant	entrails
Flying squirrel	hair
Fox	lung
Human	flesh, brain, or bones
Owl	feathers, feces, urine
Peacock	feathers
Snake	skin, flesh
Swallow	lung
Tibetan fox	urine , feces, bile
Vulture	flesh
White rhinoceros	horn
Wild horse	bones
Wild yak	heart
Wolf	stomach, dung

Although the practice is gradually becoming outdated, animal parts are still used in the production of Tibetan medicine. As you can see, very little is wasted when it comes to the production of medicine.

testament to this danger. The situation clearly indicates the need for a concerted effort on the part of all who make their living in this way to discover ways to cultivate those plants which can be grown in gardens and to find domestic substitutes for the rest. In the past, every Tibetan doctor prepared his own medicines by hand, so there was little danger of ecosystem damage. Today, however, the use of machines has altered the dynamics. Still, I found the allure of a plant collecting expedition into the Himalayas to be an intriguing prospect, a dream that I hoped to fulfill before leaving the region.

Such were my thoughts as I watched the pharmacist at work. Seeing the rilbu stockpiled so carefully along the wall reminded me of something else. The year before in Ithaca, Dr. Dawa had presented a wonderful lecture on techniques for collecting and preparing medicinal plants. Thanks to his presentation, I had some idea of how these medicines are compounded. The technique is very elaborate and understanding it thoroughly requires detailed instruction and an actual apprenticeship. Nevertheless, his lecture had given me an appreciation of the knowledge necessary to create traditional remedies.

Collecting and Preparing Medicinal Plants

Although you might not realize it while watching wild plant gatherers at work, collecting and preparing medicinal plants is as much a science as it is an art. Gatherers must have detailed knowledge about the biological characteristics of plants. They also must have a good understanding of astrology, topography, climate, and medical theory. Some of these areas are explained briefly below.

Habitat: Plants, like the diseases they are used to treat, are classified as either hot or cold (yang or yin) in nature. Medicinal plants which are considered to be cold in nature have superior healing power if they are collected in their natural environment, that is, in colder climates or at higher elevations. The converse is true of plants considered to be hot.

Time: Every plant can be divided into constituent parts. For each part—roots, stems, leaves, and fruits—there is an optimal time when harvesting is most favorable. The roots of a plant, for example, should be collected in the fall, after the top of the plant has matured and ripened. At this time, the energy of the plant has left the leaves and stems and descended into the roots, making them stronger and more vital.

Removal of Impurities: After harvesting, the coarser qualities of the plant must be removed. These elements are likened to poisons. If the plant is not thoroughly cleaned, the resulting medicine can adversely affect the wind energy, the overall strength of the body, and the constituents of the body themselves. So, for example, when roots are collected, the external bark must be removed before processing. This makes the final preparation smooth and digestible.

Drying: Plants which warm the body are dried in the sun. Plants which cool the body are dried in the shade. Chopping plants into little pieces ensures thorough drying.

Duration: Medicines must be used before they lose their healing qualities. Unlike minerals and precious stones, plants lose their special properties quickly. Medicines made from the trunks, roots, and fruits of plants can be stored for between three and four years.

Medicines from leaves can be saved only one year before their potency dissipates. If you cannot use the leaves in the first year, you can prepare a decoction which can be kept for two or three years.

Compounding: Tibetan medicines are never made from just one ingredient. Most frequently, medicines are made from several plants with similar qualities. This makes the remedies more soothing, more smooth, and easier to digest. Some may contain seventy ingredients or more, while others have only four.

The Powers of Foods and Medicines: The precise medicinal qualities of foods and drugs are determined, in part, through their tastes.

Another set of qualities associated with foods and medicines is known as "the powers." Like the tastes, powers are used to identify characteristics of edible plants which can then be compounded in suitable proportions to bring the humors back into balance. The eight major powers, described here in pairs, are: light and coarse, cool and bland, heavy and greasy, hot and sharp.

Some grains, such as millet and barley, are considered to be both heavy and cool. These properties are known to be useful in healing bones, promoting strength in the body, and improving digestive functions. But when taken in excess or to the exclusion of other dietary elements such as vegetables, they can cause an excess of phlegm.

At long last, I was ushered upstairs to see Dr. Kunsang Dorjee. Over tea and cookies, we discussed the history of his clinic and the source of the clinic's medicine. Dr. Dorjee explained that his clinic purchased its medicine from a monastery just beyond the Nepali border in Langtang, Tibet. Naturally, this meant dealing directly with the Chinese. Dr. Dorjee, however, seemed unconcerned. In fact, he suggested I visit Langtang to see for myself exactly where and how the medicines were made.

While I found the idea intriguing, I had already committed to a lengthy journey to Kalimpong in the Darjeeling district in the Bengal Hills of northeastern India.

Before we parted, Dr. Dorjee suggested I contact Dr. Gyelek Gyatso, who, he said, was more fluent in English. Dr. Gyatso had recently opened a clinic near the Great Stupa not far from where I was staying. Following this lead, I met not only Dr. Gyatso but his two students, Tenzin and Mindu. They provided a fascinating firsthand account of their medical training, which was a private apprenticeship and not instruction through one of the principle institutions such as Men Tsee Khang. This training is described in some detail in Chapter 6.

Amchi Kunsang Dorjee runs the Kunphen Clinic. Dr. Dorjee, also a Buddhist lama, kindly discussed the nature of the clinic and his work with me over tea.

AID FROM THE WEST

The longer I stayed in Nepal, the more clear it became to me that even the relatively inexpensive, natural, and nontechnological approach of Tibetan medicine could not address adequately the

medical problems of an overcrowded area like Katmandu. Despite clinics like Kunphen, diseases and health problems of all descriptions were visible everywhere.

One day, while sitting in the sunny courtyard at the Rabsel thinking about this problem, I fell into conversation with Maya Altwegg, a Swiss nurse who spends part of the year volunteering for the Rokpa clinic. *Rokpa*, one of the thousands of NGOs offering aid to the people of Nepal, is a Tibetan word meaning "help." The international organization is dedicated to helping the sick, the poor, the helpless, and the hungry in many parts of the world, including Nepal, India, and Tibet. Rokpa also adopts children and has a job skills training program for indigent mothers, who receive food, shelter, medical treatment, and education.

After hearing about these projects, I decided to tag along with Maya over the next few days as she made her rounds. One day, we met two young girls who had avoided the all-too-common fate of so many girls in this part of the world—slavery in foreign brothels. Now they were attending a small Rokpa boarding school, studying and playing as they should. Young boys studied there as well. The principal, expressing some concern, confided in me that none of his wards had yet reached puberty. After discovering that I had been an educator, he asked for suggestions about group management in the coming years. Constant vigilance and explicit education were my only recommendations.

Maya Altwegg opens the door to the Rokpa facilities in Bodhnath which she shares with Tibetan healers. Maya not only showed me this clinic but later a school for homeless children, a retraining program for destitute women, and the Rokpa soup kitchen.

I also met adult women who had not been as successful as these children in avoiding the

horrors of abject poverty and sexual slavery. Now, however, they were off the streets, practicing new trades, selling their products, and managing their own money. The Rokpa clinic, I also discovered, does extensive work with diseases among beggars and street children, treating such serious afflictions as leprosy, tuberculosis, and eye problems. The elderly were tested and fitted for glasses, children were immunized, and many found relief from the debilitating conditions so evident on the streets.

Seeing these people, once wretched and impoverished, so cheerful, healthy, and successful filled me with gratitude for the far-sighted, compassionate individuals who staff and support Rokpa and other relief agencies like it. The experience also gave me plenty to think about in evaluating the effectiveness of traditional medical practice. I found myself comparing the virtues of traditional healing and this distinctly Western approach to caregiving, which combines emergency relief, education, and Western-style medical attention. As far as I knew, Rokpa is not connected to any particular religious belief system. It is simply helping suffering people in a very practical, immediate way.

FREE CLINIC AT THE GREAT STUPA

Two weeks into my trip, I had the good fortune to see another kind of medical clinic in action. An acquaintance had mentioned that from time to time medical people, including lamas, nuns, and doctors, organize special street clinics to make certain that the community receives at least rudimentary medical care. Such a clinic sprang up late one day beside the Great Stupa of Bodhnath. I had been sitting in a restaurant reviewing my notes when I happened to glance out the restaurant window. There in the street, I noticed a large crowd gathering. The people were quiet, respectful, and formed an orderly line. By early evening their numbers had grown to over a hundred.

All ages were represented among those waiting for treatment. They stood in a semicircle around the doctor, who sat at a small picnic table, his back to a brick wall. Monks dressed in yellow and ochre robes and one nun in comparatively subdued colors were assisting. They were organizing medicines, dealing with paperwork, and generally managing the crowd.

Medicines of all types sat on the table. Some pills were colored orange, while others were white. Still others were distinctly Tibetan, small brownish pills stored in jars. The monks also dispensed a Western-looking bottled medicine. Noting the variety of remedies being offered, I realized that it was not only possible for Eastern and Western medical practices to merge but that it was actually happening. To see people being treated in this way was a great relief. The

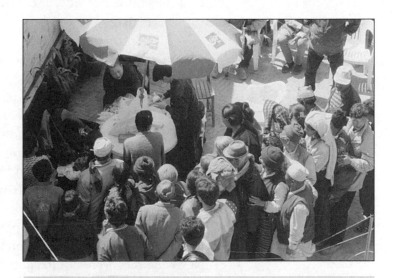

The "picnic table" clinic at the Great Stupa of Bodhnath, dispensed both Tibetan and Western medicine.

suffering caused by disease in this part of the world is difficult for Westerners to imagine. Eradicating disease will require the best efforts of all medical people, whatever their educational backgrounds.

Every traveler to this region is warned about the danger of contracting hepatitis, jaundice, typhoid, meningitis, polio, malaria, or any one of a number of other diseases, each one notorious for taking its toll in human misery. One statistic claims that of every two people in nearby India, one tests positive for exposure to tuberculosis. Naturally, before leaving, I had been certain to take every possible inoculation, enough to make a pin cushion of my arm.

The street clinic continued far into the evening. Toddlers, youth,

the elderly, adults by themselves or carrying infants, everyone in need, it seemed, was present. They waited patiently and quietly. People stood side by side, pushed up against each other. One elderly woman, propped up by adults on either side, gazed out into the crowd as if to see who else might be there.

After watching for a while, I noticed something peculiar. Sadly, the street children, the beggars, the lepers, the disabled, and the homeless did not seem to be present. Many of these wretched people conducted their begging business on this very same spot. Now, however, they were curiously absent. The people attending the street clinic on that evening all looked reasonably well dressed and well kept. Though I had no way of knowing whether the treatment being offered was free, from what I could see, money did not change hands.

At the far side of the circle of patients, a dog lay motionless on the ground. Many strays had found sanctuary within the walls of the Great Stupa. While they were not liked, they were tolerated, due to the Buddhist veneration for life in all its forms. Pedestrians gave this animal a wide berth, walking carefully around it. The dog must have known that it was perfectly safe, for it appeared relaxed and comfortable. Judging from the mange on the dog's hide, it was abundantly clear that, as the Buddhists say, suffering is not confined to the human population but is endemic to all sentient beings.

CHAPTER FIVE

A Melding of Healing Traditions

In certain seasons, night falls early in Katmandu, and I adopted the habit of retiring just after dark and rising with the dawn. The early morning sun felt good as I sat on some steps watching the Tibetan community awaken. Nearby, a storekeeper swept the street in front of her shop. Clouds of dust swirled around us, and the sunbeams illuminated a myriad of tiny particles. Since my arrival, I had learned to find metaphors in everything.

In the middle of a stroke, the woman suddenly stopped, bent down, and plucked something from beneath her broom. Walking a few steps to a nearby flowerbox, she stooped and dropped into it a small winged insect.

This was real Buddhism in action. Compassion is a way of life here, and according to the teachings, it must be extended to all beings, great or insignificant. A story is told that in one of his previous lifetimes, the Buddha was born as a noble and compassionate prince. While strolling in a park one day, he came upon a starving tigress and her five cubs, scarcely a week old. Recognizing that his own destiny was to die himself someday, the prince decided to offer his own life to save the beast and her young. The willing surrender of his own precious life, he reasoned, would generate enough positive karma to carry him out of the realm of suffering and into enlightenment.

81

Though the prince offered himself to her claws, the tigress was too weak from starvation to attack him. So taking a sharp bamboo stem, the future Buddha cut his own throat. At the smell of fresh blood, the tigress revived and devoured her willing victim.

No similar mercy is shown to animals in the West. Mangy dogs are rescued from their misery, only to be gassed a few days later. A starving tigress and her cubs might be fed, but they are likely to be auctioned off the next day to the highest bidder at a rare animal auction. And what of the winged insect?

Compassion lies at the heart of Buddhist philosophy and is the core of Tibetan healing practice. My wrestling match with the Bodhisattva Vow during the Medicine Buddha initiation had taught me that much. This fundamental element can clearly be seen in all of the Buddha's teachings. Further generations of scholars and practitioners have taken these teachings and woven them seamlessly into all of their arts, especially healing practice.

This integration can be seen clearly in Tibetan imagery. For example, though his iconography is different, the Medicine Buddha is identical in nature with the historical Buddha, Shakyamuni. But when a thangka is painted of the Medicine Buddha, the artist wishes to emphasize certain of the Buddha's qualities to the exclusion of others.

The Buddha, it is said, manifested in many forms, including one devoted especially to healing. Since the two beings are inseparable, everything taught by Shakyamuni is reflected in Medicine Buddha philosophy. The reverse is also true, and so Shakyamuni is always thought of as the supreme physician.

As Tibetan scholars freely admit, there is no historical evidence to indicate that Shakyamuni was actually a doctor. The Buddha did reason, though, that the ultimate source of our physical ailments was the psychological afflictions of hatred, attachment, and ignorance. He

offered a cure as well—the teachings of the dharma. For this reason, Shakyamuni is often referred to as the Great Physician and is considered to be the source of Tibetan healing arts. But, even though the Buddha taught the secrets of healing in the form of Medicine Buddha, he did not create them. According to the scriptures, the secrets of healing have always existed.

The Nature of Enlightenment

The teachings tell us that the ultimate awareness a human being can attain is the full enlightenment reached by Shakyamuni Buddha beneath the Bodhi tree. I have often wondered about the precise meaning of enlightenment. One day, I asked Khensur Rinpoche to describe it. "Even after you have conquered the three poisons, ignorance, aversion, and desire," he told me, "your mind is still stained. It is as if you had placed a clove of garlic in a jar of oil. Even after you remove the garlic, the scent remains." The enlightened mind, I concluded, has neither garlic nor smell!

INFLUENCES FROM ANCIENT TRADITIONS

Long before Tibetan lamas and physicians constructed their masterful system of healing arts, the practices they came to rely on were in daily use. In fact, in various states of development, similar healing techniques had been used for centuries, even millennia, throughout Asia. Many ideas had even been fully refined and put to use in the comprehensive healing system known as Ayurveda, India's indigenous medical science.

The roots of Ayurveda extend far into the past, into the shadowy

Vedic period of Indian history. Some aspects of the tradition are, perhaps, four thousand years old. Over the centuries, Ayurvedic principles concerning health and enlightenment were perfected by the Rishis, India's fabled poets and adepts. Through their meditations, the Rishis gleaned vital information about humanity and its relationship to the universe. From these beginnings, Ayurveda grew into the advanced health-care system practiced today around the world.

An important source of information on the early healing practices of ancient India is a text known as the *Atharva-Veda*, or the "Knowledge of Magic Formulas." A collection of 731 psalms, it is one of the earliest texts ever written on the subject of healing.

The text of the *Atharva-Veda* offers us a window into a culture long vanished, one rich in sacred imagery and metaphor. In the Vedic worldview, divine forces seemed very close by and could easily be accessed through prayer and magic. The Rishis communicated with deities, demons, animals, and plants, and they set down what they learned in poetic form. Over the centuries, these verses have become somewhat cryptic and difficult for us to understand. Still, the documents clearly suggest a world very dif-

Evidence for the continuing influence of magical healing practices in the region is everywhere. The Tooth God can be propitiated by nailing a small coin to a mass of hundreds of other coins on a particular wall in a narrow alley near Chhetrapati Square, Katmandu. A small opening smeared with red dye suggests a mouth in pain. Tooth-related infections are a major cause of illness and even death in undeveloped countries.

ferent from our own in which people, plants, animals, and even diseases lived in intimate relationship. The verses of the Rishis describe this relationship. They note such phenomena as omens and suggest the special mantras and spells which are antidotes for particular illnesses.

A Vedic healer might address an incantation such as the following to an assembly of herbs, petitioning them to restore an individual to health: "Those that are brown, and that are bright, the red and the spotted, the swarthy, the black herbs, all [of them] do we address. Let them save this man from the *yaksma* [consumption] sent by the gods—the plants of which heaven has been the father, earth the mother, ocean the root."

Later, in the same psalm, the poet/doctor requests assistance from all of the herbs working in consort: "Rich in flowers, rich in shoots, rich in fruits, also those lacking fruits—like joint mothers, let them milk unto this man in order to [restore] his freedom from harm [illness]."[7]

Vedic texts refer to many of the same ideas adopted later by Indian Buddhists and still later by Tibetan medical practitioners. For instance, the *Atharva-Veda* clearly points to the mind poisons as the source of disease: "If it is born out of desire, of aversion, of the heart, the *balasa* [another term for consumption] from thy heart, thy limbs, we expel out [of thee] by incantation."[8] As in Tibetan Buddhist belief, desire and aversion are cited here as causes for disease. These verses were recorded at least a thousand years before the birth of Shakyamuni Buddha. And even before they were

This photo depicts an Ayurvedic remedy, with its ingredients in preprocessed form. Two of the four ingredients in this compound, *Terminalia chebula* and *Terminalia belerica* are varieties of the Myrobalan tree. The formula here is used as a remedy for diarrhea.

written down, they were part of a venerable oral tradition.

As in Tibetan healing, the Ayurvedic system of diagnosis and prescription is based on restoring the balance between the human body and certain universal laws. For example, Ayurveda sees illness as the direct result of violating the natural laws which govern our inner self, known as the Atman. This indwelling self is the source of our health, and it is only by attending to it, that is, to the tripartite nature of our being—body, mind, and spirit together—that we achieve liberation from illness, disease, and even misfortune. Though Tibetan philosophy denies the exisistence of an indwelling self, it does point to *ma-rig-pa*— the ignorant state of consciousness—as the root of all problems and illness.

Mantras are found everywhere—carved into rocks, engraved on bells and prayer wheels, painted on any available surface. This mantra carving is found at the monastery of the Tamang Healer, Dinchen Rinpoche, in Mongpoo, West Bengal. It was brought there as a holy object from a distant place to sanctify the grounds.

During the Buddhist period in India, roughly 500 BC to 500 AD, Ayurveda reached its peak of development. Its physicians practiced surgery and dentistry, set bones, and compiled a rich index of healing herbs. The healing methodology also included a vast repertoire of mantras and incantations to avoid or cure diseases and difficulties of all types.

Mantras have many other uses. Among the most fascinating to me was as a means of long-distance communcation.

Long-Distance Communication through Flowers

Dinchen Rinpoche, also known as the Tamang Healer, is a well-known Tantric adept. Although he has built a number of monasteries, one of his largest is located in Mongpoo, a tiny village in the low-lying jungles of West Bengal. His monastery is home to the elderly, homeless children, the sick, and quite a number of stray dogs and cats as well.

According to tradition, many strange and powerful abilities can be gained through the practice of Tantric meditation. The Mongpoo Rinpoche told me about one of these:

Peter: Many people in the West really love flowers. But none of them know how to communicate over distance using them. Yesterday I watched the Cintury Mataji [a Hindu woman healer and priestess in Darjeeling] send you a message by means of an acacia blossom. Would you discuss this ability?

Rinpoche: This is one of the really old, beautiful forms of communication. The secret lies in the mantra you are using. You project your thought into the flower and whomever the message is intended for can hear your thought out of the flower. This technique is only possible for a person of very high level of concentration and meditation.

You can use flowers but you can also use other media as well. Sometimes my disciples are far away. When I need to communicate

with them, I might take some rice flakes and place my mantra into them. Then I throw the flakes into the wind, and my disciples will be able to understand exactly what I am trying to say. Using the flower is a very old tradition. The moment the fragrance is inhaled, the message will be transmitted.

Wandering monks preserved the ancient texts from destruction at the hands of the Moslems, often at great cost to their personal safety and health. Indeed, even within living memory they have had to continue to carry texts to safe havens to preserve them from destruction at the hands of the Communist Chinese.

The Ayurvedic tradition flourished in India until the Islamic invasions from the north in the late twelfth century. The invaders systematically destroyed virtually everything Buddhist and prevented its further development in the land of its origin. Indeed, the eradication of Buddhist traditions in India was so thorough that most aspects of Ayurvedic science were nearly extinguished. Fortunately, its healing wisdom was preserved in Tibet, where Indian monks had wandered or traveled by invitation, carrying with them many of its texts. Tibetan monks, too, had traveled to India specifically to study Ayurvedic and other sciences and to return with the knowledge to their native land.

When texts were first carried into Tibet, however, long before the Islamic invasion of India, the Tibetans faced a very special problem. In order for the imported texts to be preserved and studied, they first needed to be translated from the original Sanskrit. This was not an easy task, since in the seventh century Tibetans did not have a written language. So

precious were the Buddhist teachings brought over the mountains that a written form of Tibetan was invented for the sole purpose of translating the religious and medical ideas and other sciences arriving from India. Since that time, Tibetan scholars have thoroughly scrutinized these ideas and subjected them to exhaustive debate and commentary. The result is a vast collection of texts which deal with almost every conceivable aspect of Buddhist thought.

EARLY TIBETAN MEDICAL HISTORY

Tradition has it that the oldest Tibetan medical writings date from the period of King Songtsen Gampo, who reigned in Tibet almost 1300 years ago. Information about the early history of Tibetan healing can be found in a text written in 1702 by Jaya Pandita a Mongolian scholar who studied medicine and pharmacology in various monasteries in Central Tibet. Well versed in the healing arts, he even compounded his own medicines according to traditional formulae.

Jaya Pandita traced the development of medicine in Tibet over the thousand-year period between the seventh and seventeenth centuries AD. His description of the period makes clear that there were times when Tibet experienced something of a medical and spiritual renaissance. During these periods, medical knowledge was actively sought out, and scholarship was openly encouraged. Especially notable is the open-mindedness of many of Tibet's rulers, who often personally sponsored the gathering of intellectual, cultural, and scientific ideas from many countries.

Consider, for example, several of the great Tibetan kings who ruled during roughly a hundred-year period beginning in the middle of the seventh century. King Songtsen Gampo (619-650) married a Chinese princess, Onzhing Kongjo, who brought with her to Tibet at least one medical text from China. One work was translated into Tibetan by the scholars Hashang Mahadeva and Dharmakosha.

Three physicians, Bharadhvaja from India, Henwen Hangde from China, and Galenas from Persia, were then invited to Tibet by King Songtsen Gampo to add their contributions to Tibetan medical knowledge. Each translated several important medical texts well known in their native lands. These works were subsequently published in Tibetan in seven volumes.

Until the time of the "Magical King" Dusong Mangpoje Lung (676–704), these books comprised the only medical library in Tibet. However, when Jangcha Habon, the son of King Tride Songtsen Mesagthsom (705–755), married the Chinese princess Kyimsang Konjo, she brought with her a number of new mathematical and medical works. These, as well as many other scholarly texts, were then translated.

The next ruler, King Trisong Detsen (755–797) invited many prominent figures from distant lands to continue the work of building a great medical library. Shantigarbha from India and Guhyabadzra from Kashmir arrived. Three scholars made the trek from China, Tongsum Gangba, Hashang Bala, and Hariba. From Iran came Halashanti, and from Grugu, the Turkish settlements in East Turkestan, came Sengdo Ochen. Khyoma Rutse from Dolpo and Dhanashila from Nepal were also invited.

The scholars set to work with local translators, and when they finished, an enormous number of medical texts were available in Tibetan. According to Jaya Pandita, these included six texts from India, nine from China, three from Kashmir, five from Iran, six from Grugu, four from Dolpo, and four from Nepal.

Imagine the difficulties involved in this endeavor. Tibet's capital, Lhasa, lies at an altitude of 15,000 feet. Although trade routes were well established, travel time was measured in weeks or even months. These scholars undertook projects which they knew would take many years— even, perhaps, the remainder of their lives. Given all of this, their efforts in collecting and preserving the medical knowledge of the time seem nothing short of heroic.

The Nectar Essence of the Eight Branches of Healing

The most important collection of Tibetan medical lore is *The Gyushi*, a work of exactly 156 chapters. The full title of this masterpiece in Tibetan is elaborate and poetic: "The Ambrosia Heart Tantra: The Secret Oral Teachings on the Nectar Essence of the Eight Branches of Healing."

Five thousand nine hundred verses in length, *The Gyushi* is written in a secret, poetic language intelligible only to initiates. As legend has it, after the initial transmission of the text by Shakyamuni Buddha, it was passed down to various disciples. Sometime toward the end of the eighth century, the well-known Kashmiri pandit, Chandranandana, gave a written Sanskrit form of *The Gyushi* to Vairochana, the translator. Vairochana, incidentally, was one of the first few Tibetan monks to be ordained into Buddhism. In fact, he was a direct disciple of Padmasambhava.

Vairochana translated this sacred text into Tibetan. He then presented his work to King Trisong Detsen and Padmasambhava. Vairochana also passed *The Gyushi* on to the Yuthog Yontan Gonpo the Elder (708–833) who was not only one of nine court physicians but was to become one of Tibet's most scholarly and accomplished physicians of the eighth and early ninth centuries. He died at the age of 125.

The Gyushi

*T*he Gyushi is presumed to be the textual record of the discourse offered by Shakyamuni Buddha on the subject of medicine and health. This passage is translated directly

from that text. It discusses the fundamental relationship of the five universal elements to the growth and development of the body.

"If the karma is not present, the consciousness cannot enter (the fertilized egg). Without earth, there cannot be formation. Without water, it is not possible to unite (semen and egg). Without fire, there will be no maturation, and without wind, no growth. Without space, there cannot be room for growth."[9]

Tradition has it, though, that humankind was not yet ready to receive the teachings contained in *The Gyushi*. As a consequence, the texts were secreted away by Padmasambhava himself, or at least at his request, inside a pillar of the Samye Monastery. Such hidden treasures, intended for later rediscovery, are known as *terma*. Though the exact date of *The Gyushi*'s rediscovery is not known, the text remained in hiding for over two hundred years.

Atisha and the Kadampa Sect

Tibetan rulers did not always welcome Buddhism, and there were periods when Buddhism was suppressed in Tibet. Still, even during these periods, new ideas made their way into the mountain stronghold. Tibetan monks, for example, often made their way into India to learn what they could of the dharma and of Ayurveda. As well, wandering monks and adepts from India sometimes traveled into Tibet voluntarily to teach, passing on what they knew of the medical and spiritual sciences.

In periods of political liberalism, still others arrived by invitation. Such was the case of Atisha, the Indian saint, scholar, and physician, born of royal descent. In AD 1038, Atisha, by that time an aging man, left the sacred Vikramasila Monastery in Bengal and journeyed to Tibet at the request of two rulers, Yeshe Yod and Jangchub Yöd. With him, he brought his own writings, including *The Heart of Life,* an important work on Ayurvedic medicine.

A renowned Buddhist teacher, scholar, and physician, Atisha founded the Kadampa sect of Tibetan Buddhism, from which grew the Gelugpa or "Yellow Hat" school of the current and all previous Dalai Lamas. He is revered as a great physician and saint, whose knowledge and influence helped preserve and develop the dharma in Tibet.

Oral history maintains that Atisha also taught a form of the Medicine Buddha meditation practice and taught *The Gyushi* to Tibetan physicians from the Nethang Drolma Lhakhang Monastery with which he was closely associated. In fact, he later died in this monastery. In passing, it is worth mentioning that although many monasteries and other Tibetan treasures were destroyed during the Communist Chinese cultural revolution, Nethang Drolma Lhakhang survived relatively intact, with most of its precious artifacts preserved. It seems that the Chinese premier, Chou En Lai, prevented its destruction at the request of the government of the country today known as Bangladesh.

The holy relics saved from destruction include such objects as two clay Guardian Kings who have stood watch over the entrance for a thousand years and the stone grinder used by Yuthog Yontan Gonpo to grind his medicines. As well, there are many irreplaceable objects, especially the stacks of ancient manuscripts that comprise the Kangyur, the set of works reputed to be the sermons of the Buddha.

The Revision of The Gyushi

As already noted, *The Gyushi* was placed inside a pillar at the Samye monastery for safe keeping until a future time. Some say the *terton* or "treasure discoverer" was the monk Trapa Ngonshe (1012–1090), who rediscovered the text in 1038. Others believe that the text was found

somewhat later by Yuthog Yontan Gonpo the Younger (1121–1203), the descendant of Yuthog the Elder who initially received the teaching some four hundred years earlier.

Regardless, it was Yuthog the Younger who studied it and is credited with its revision to accommodate distinctly Tibetan and regional knowledge such as the Tibetan pharmacopoeia. Since the original Indian version of the Sanskrit text has never been found, however, it is difficult to say exactly what it did contain.

Born to a royal family in Central Tibet in 1121, Yuthog the Younger was a gifted healer as well as a passionate student. While still a very young man, he traveled throughout the mountainous regions of Tibet in search of those rare individuals, such as Dardag from Central Tibet, who might have the knowledge to help him interpret *The Gyushi*. Yuthog also made the arduous trek to India six times in pursuit of traditional medical knowledge. As a consequence of his efforts, the practice of medicine in Tibet was further refined.

Shortly after his time, the Islamic conquest of India resulted in the destruction not only of Buddhist practices but also of much of the vast Indian medical and scientific tradition. It is believed that Yuthog's enthusiasm for study did much to preserve the Ayurvedic aspects of this heritage. By the end of the twelfth century, the vast influx of knowledge into Tibet had all but stopped. Still, the Tibetans had acquired a fabulous medical tradition, and they devoted their finest efforts to preserving and enhancing it.

Under the guidance of carefully trained lamas who recognized their lasting value, ideas from the medical systems of China, India, Persia, Mongolia, Bon and other systems had been integrated into a structure known today as the Medicine Buddha tradition. Relatively safe for the time being in the isolated mountain kingdom, these ideas were preserved and nurtured for another eight hundred years until yet another invasion threatened their existence.

Dr. Dakpa Lectures on The Gyushi

The four books of *The Gyushi* are still studied closely by Tibetan doctors. As these texts are considered to be the recorded words of the Buddha, they are believed to be infallible. The notion of infallibility is an odd concept to the Western mind, turned as it is toward scientific method. It becomes even more peculiar when put to the test.

During one of his lectures at Ithaca, Dr. Dakpa described an exhaustive search he had undertaken through modern microbiology textbooks. He was looking for a photograph of a microorganism which a few lines in the ancient *Gyushi* states arises from wrong conduct and wrong views.

The Gyushi describes the organism as shaped something like a lizard, with a large mouth and a snakelike tail. Its body has many limbs including wings which it uses to travel everywhere. It invades human hosts through the orifices and moves through the body by means of the bloodstream. When it finds a weak organ, it takes hold and gradually begins to damage it. Perhaps, said the doctor, this organism is so small and subtle, it is yet unknown to science.

Though Dr. Dakpa had not yet found his microorganism, at some point in the future, he told us cheerfully, he was certain that he would. Given his tenacity and faith, I had no doubt of his success.

SHAMANISM AND DIVINATION IN HEALING PRACTICE

A Tibetan thankga painting illustrates how diagnosis by divination might work. The man to the east of the tortoise shell is urinating onto the shell. The system of using tortoise shells for divination is probably Chinese in origin, since similar techniques have been practiced in China for millennia. A divinatory template consisting of nine squares on a grid is superimposed over the shell. Each direction corresponds to one of nine spirits which can affect a person's health. These spirits, called *sadak,* are of Bon origin.

In addition to importing healing knowledge from India, China, and other cultures in the region, the Tibetan healing system incorporated the wisdom of its own indigenous shamanic culture, the Bon tradition. Sortilege (casting lots), astrology, and other methods of divination were commonly used to predict the future, diagnose illness, and determine appropriate treatment. Such techniques are still taught in contemporary courses in Tibetan medicine.

Severe medical problems, often of a psychological nature, are sometimes understood to be related to "possession" by a spirit or demon. In order to prescribe an appropriate healing ritual, it is first necessary to determine which type of demon is at the root of the problem.

The Nine Spirits which Cause Illness

EAST: related to people and both male and female demons

SOUTHEAST: related to the gods and their wrath

SOUTH: related to male ancestors and the demons associated with property

SOUTHWEST: location of the cemetery and its associated fiends

WEST: location of the household and harms from the Nagas (powerful snake spirits)

NORTHWEST: the earth deity and associated plague-causing demons

NORTH: related to male descendents and the demons from the female line of descent

NORTHWEST: related to demons and the harm they cause

CENTER: related to self and harm from infectious demons

In his wonderful book, *The Nine Ways of Bon*, David Snellgrove translates a number of folios which he estimates to be about four hundred years old. The Bon tradition itself dates to an antique period in the history of this region, to the eighth century at least and probably earlier. But over the course of centuries, the cultural exchange between Bon and Buddhist religious cultures was very liberal. Eventually, many of the central ideas and practices became thoroughly intertwined. Clear

evidence of this mingling is found in the later Bon texts which seem to depend heavily on Buddhist doctrine.

These early texts describe a religion that relied on indigenous magic and ritual. Some of these ancient techniques are similar to those still in use today.

The Nine Ways of Bon

The following text speaks of urinalysis, observation of the channels, and the study of general appearance as diagnostic tools. It suggests the worship of Vaidurya, an emanation of Shakyamuni Buddha in his healing form. These ideas clearly reflect the influence of Buddhism on Bon traditions. The following passage is taken from "The Way of the Shen of Prediction":

"He should worship the King Be-du-rgya-'od (Vaidurya) and his eight fellow Buddhas, gods of medicine. Then he should diagnose the major and minor causes in all that can be seen, and identify the disease by diagnosis of the connecting channels. Diagnose from the urine what is of benefit and what is of harm. Diagnose from the appearance all signs of death and signs of cure. Thus identifying the disease. Heat or cold, phlegm, or bile, or some combination, the medicine is then applied, cooling, warming, equalizing, powder, pills, or syrup, potion, ointment, or butter-mould. Medicine for every man must fit the disease."[10]

As we have seen, many of the ideas discussed in this passage are alive in Tibetan medical practice. Problems are still diagnosed according to indications of the urine and by the general appearance of the patient. Omens and signs are still read to determine health. Medicines and foods are still thought of as either warming or cooling in their effects and, all prescriptions must suit the individual exactly.

Of course, all of these ideas cannot rightly be said to be Bon in origin. Here again, the influence of Ayurveda and possibly the Chinese system are clear. While the Bon healing tradition did contribute its own unique information, like the Tibetan tradition, it, too, is indebted to prior traditions.

FAMILY HEALING TRADITIONS

Another significant source of Tibetan medical information is family traditions. Not all medical advances took place in large centers under official sponsorship. Very significant traditions arose within various families living in outlying provinces, such as Kham, Amdo, and Tsang.

Here, a number of distinct practices came to life and developed over the course of centuries. Handed down from parents to children, these practices formed much of the medical infrastructure for the vast, sparsely populated countryside. This heritage, though scattered widely, may in the future furnish students of Tibetan medicine with a vast untapped resource for study.

Sometime later on my journey, in Northern India, I had the good fortune to meet a healer who worked within a family lineage tradition. While he did not practice Tibetan medicine, he had inherited his unique medical practice and his special healing abilities along a four-generation family line. His work, officially recognized by the Indian government, offered me some insight into the importance of family medical traditions.

CHAPTER SIX

The Training of a
Tibetan Healer

Historically, training to become a Tibetan healer was a long and arduous process. In the institutions, training could take nine years. In family traditions, training might take much longer, and complete mastery required as many as ten additional years of regular practice. No wonder Tibetan doctors were so renowned. Becoming a master of the art might take twenty years—not unheard of by contemporary standards, but certainly a long education.

After fleeing Tibet, the Fourteenth Dalai Lama received permission from the Indian government to settle in Dharamsala, a small Himalayan mountain town. The Tibetan refugee community was in desperate need of medical attention. In 1961, two years after arriving in India, the Dalai Lama took steps to preserve Tibet's precious healing tradition. He founded the Tibetan Medical and Astrological Institute, which initially operated as two educational establishments, one for medicine and one for astrology. The Institute's purpose was to train doctors and astrologers, to rebuild Tibet's famed libraries of medical and astrological knowledge, and to interest the rest of the world in these practices. Five years later, the two organizations merged and became Men Tsee Khang.

It was farsighted of the Dalai Lama and his advisors to undertake this initiative, since the next decade was to see the destruction of great numbers of monasteries and other cultural institutions. This resulted

in the loss of invaluable and sometimes irreplaceable cultural and medical information in Tibet itself. As well, the murder of a sixth of the Tibetan population—1.2 million people—at the hands of the People's Liberation Army and the Red Guards took the lives of a great many learned monks, many of whom were expert in Tibetan healing.

Originally, this new institution tried to train physicians as they had been taught at Men Tsee Khang, founded in 1916, in Lhasa. But the immediacy of the medical needs of the refugee population outweighed the value of a strictly traditional curriculum. A streamlined training schedule made new physicians available to work with the Tibetan community in exile within five or six years.

Mrs. Choezom is a senior astrologer with Men Tsee Khang. She was the first woman in exile to graduate with proficiency in astrology and higher Sanskrit grammar. Here, she prepares a traditional astrological chart for me.

These doctors, however, did not have the traditional depth of understanding of the medical arts and practiced with only limited knowledge of astrology and pharmacology. These shortcomings were amended, in part at least, in an interesting way—with instruction in Western anatomy and biochemistry. From time to time, these medical students also had the chance to travel outside of India, giving them the opportunity to introduce their subject to the world and to learn something of Western healing methods.

Tibetan astrology is divided into two categories, elemental astrology and astronomy. The five elements, the twelve animal signs, the nine numbers of the magic square, and the eight traditional Chinese trigrams are all used in conjunction with the date of a person's birth to determine negative and positive influences and to make inferences about the future. During the interview, the astrologer typically discusses four general categories: personal life force, general health, finances, and prospects for success.

One young Tibetan doctor in Delhi told me about his own training and how the new curriculum had affected him. As a result of the compressed course of study, he said, he knew little about pharmacology. Because his academic standing was not high enough, he had not been invited to undertake this difficult subject. Only a few top students, perhaps one or two each year, were invited to learn the process of manufacturing medicines. Though he practiced as a Tibetan doctor, he was dependent on others to manufacture medicine for him, a situation he regretted.

After a certain period of study, some student physicians apprentice to a doctor in private practice. Others who study with Men Tsee Khang itself begin work in a Men Tsee Khang medical clinic. These branch clinics have been established in all Tibetan settlements and in most of the major cities of Nepal and India. At this time, there are about forty such clinics.

At their finest, Tibetan doctors are far more than medical technicians. The best have integrated Tibetan medical principles with a deep understanding of Buddhist philosophy. They are proficient in the Medicine Buddha *sadhana*, the ritual that animates the practice. While many Tibetan doctors are skilled in the physical science of healing, fewer today are as knowledgeable in this spiritual sense, which is truly unfortunate.

MINDU AND TENZIN'S STORY

Dr. Kunsang Dorjee of the Kunphen Clinic in Chhetrapati had recommended that I seek out Dr. Gyelek Gyatso, who ran a medical clinic in Bodhnath. When I followed up on this helpful suggestion, I was fortunate to meet Mindu Dorje and Tenzin Lobsang. Both young men were

studying medicine under Dr. Gyatso. At one time, Dr. Gyatso had worked for Men Tsee Khang, but he had recently purchased this medical clinic from a doctor who was known by many. So, though he himself was new to the neighborhood, his private practice was already well established. I had come to the clinic that morning hoping to meet Dr. Gyatso personally, but he was out on his rounds, making house calls.

Tenzin, a Tibetan, spoke little English. Mindu, a Bhutanese, was quite fluent. Both wore the ochre robes of Buddhist monks. After some initial conversation, Mindu and I realized we held something in common. Dr. Dawa, the Tibetan doctor who had examined me in Ithaca and who had inspired my trip to Nepal and India had also instructed Mindu. Mindu had studied with Dr. Dawa in Lhasa. With that link established, Mindu opened up and told me his story.

Mindu had studied medicine for a number of years at a monastery in Bhutan. Although he had done well, he had not ranked among the best students. Eventually, the Abbot asked him to find some means to continue his study privately. After a long search, he found two sponsors, one a high-ranking officer in the Bhutanese military; the other, the King of Bhutan's mother.

Desperate for information, I shamelessly interrupted these two students in the midst of their studies.

Under the patronage of these two champions, Mindu made his way to Bodhnath. There he met Dr. Gyatso, his present teacher, who was helping him complete his training for a tuition fee. Tenzin had also studied at a number of monasteries, both inside Tibet and out. Now he, too, was studying with Dr. Gyatso.

On that morning, the two friends were discussing ideas from several medical texts. Mindu was preparing for his final exam, which he would take within the week. If he passed, he would be able to continue his studies—a final year of training and internship before becoming a fully qualified doctor.

The test itself would take six days. Eighty people were registered for treatment that week, and Mindu would examine and prescribe for each of them. On his patients' recommendation, he said, he would become a physician. Otherwise, he would have to try again another year.

In the fall, shortly after the monsoons but before the winter, Dr. Gyatso would take Mindu and Tenzin into the mountains in search of medicinal plants. He would teach them how to identify, gather, and prepare the plants. Later, after their journey home, they would dry, powder, compound, and bless the medicine.

When I asked him what he would do when he graduated, Mindu grew silent. Then, speaking quietly, he said that his greatest wish was to return to his monastery in Bhutan and instruct the younger students. Above all, he wished to serve his Abbot and make him proud of his former student's accomplishments.

After warning me not to go out at night—it was very dangerous in this town—and suggesting I buy a mask to shield my lungs from the acrid pollution hovering over the main streets, we parted company. I left behind firm promises that one day, if possible, I would visit Mindu in Bhutan and that I would send him his photograph as soon as possible. Several days later, I almost passed him in the street without recognizing him. The air filtration system he wore covered nearly his entire face. By this time, I was wearing a similar get-up. We laughed aloud and then, as I walked away, he reminded me once again about sending his picture.

WHAT TO LOOK FOR IN A TIBETAN MEDICAL DOCTOR

If you are considering a visit to a Tibetan doctor, it is a good idea to seek out a knowledgeable person to help you in your selection. Take the time to discuss the personal and professional qualities of the Tibetan doctor you have in mind. At its finest, Tibetan medicine is a deeply spiritual practice. For this reason, the personal habits and spiritual attitudes of the doctor you are considering should play a part in your choice.

Find out in advance about the diagnostic and treatment procedures used by the doctor. A thorough visit will include a urine exam, pulse diagnosis, interview, and extensive visual observation. The doctor will study your tongue, coloration, smell, and so on. The best doctors will have a standard way of letting Western patients know what to expect and how to prepare for the examination.

Also ask how much time you will be spending with the doctor. Some doctors are in such demand that they see more than a hundred patients every day. A visit of only five to ten minutes is unlikely to be very useful.

If possible, visit the clinic in advance and observe its working style for yourself. Ask about the clinic's reputation and read any available introductory literature. Tibetan medical clinics in the West often ask patients to fill out a questionnaire in advance of the first visit. This ensures that the doctor has some personal information about the patient. However, Western-style documentation is not the norm in India and Nepal, even today. In fact, it has only been in this decade that Tibetan doctors have begun keeping written records of client visits.

Often Tibetan physicians will set up temporary clinics when they travel in the West. However, the exam you receive from a touring doctor may not be as thorough as one in a well-established clinic. For instance, urinalysis can be problematic for tour organizers, as patients need to be informed beforehand about the preparatory procedures for

this test. Moreover, patients often arrive knowing little or nothing about Tibetan medical practice. This means that at least part of the interview will be devoted to discussing core ideas rather than to actual diagnosis and prescription.

Be sure to ask if you will be able to see the doctor again or if he has a way of providing follow-up care and answering questions. If the physician is on tour, his schedule may already be full, and there are no guarantees that the doctor will return to your area in the future.

A Warning about Allergic Reactions

A Western assistant traveling with a Tibetan doctor related the following story about Tibetan medicine pills:

"Once I was in London assisting a Tibetan physician. A patient developed a serious allergic reaction with high fever after taking a precious pill. It was our last day in the city, and the message reached Rinpoche only a few hours before departure. Advice could be given, since the doctor had not left. But what would have happened otherwise?"

"I have also seen allergic reactions, such as red skin rashes, due to the effects of a particular herb. Because the medications are always combinations of ingredients, it is often impossible to distinguish which of them caused the reaction. In such cases, all medication should be stopped immediately and, if possible, the patient should consult with the Tibetan doctor."

Some Tibetan doctors fill prescriptions by mail. If your condition changes and the doctor is not present to assess these changes, the pre-

scription cannot be adjusted accordingly. All medicines may become harmful if the dosages and combinations are not updated periodically.

Also consider the possibility of an allergic reaction. Advocates of Tibetan medicine frequently claim that Tibetan medicine pills are safe, because they contain only natural ingredients. But some Tibetan medicinal formulas contain well over a hundred different materials. Since even one of these ingredients can produce a dangerous reaction in sensitive individuals, the doctor should be available for post-treatment consultation.

Despite these concerns, there is no question that Tibetan physicians deserve their fame. As their reputation continues to spread, people worldwide are taking ever greater interest in the practice. In response, some Tibetan doctors now make regular tours, traveling thousands of miles and accepting whatever clients come their way.

Should you be interested in consulting a Tibetan doctor visiting your area, the following guidelines will help you prepare for your visit.

How to Prepare for a Visit to a Tibetan Doctor

There are two stages to preparing for a visit to a Tibetan doctor. The first takes place during the three days before the consultation. The second deals with the day of the exam itself.

Advance Preparation

1. During the three days prior to your visit, try to moderate your activities. In general, avoid alcohol, meat, strong tea or coffee,

excessive sexual activity, lack of sleep, over-exertion at work or play, traveling, or any other activity that might cause unusual stress on your body. Ideally, you should be relaxed and calm for several days before you visit the doctor.

Major upsets can interfere with the physician's diagnosis. Emotional disturbances may manifest as imbalances among the five elements. The consequent disharmony may be reflected in both the pulse and the urine diagnosis. This might direct the doctor's attention away from actual problems.

2. Certain foods, such as beets, carrots, and vitamin supplements may discolor urine. Since urinalysis relies on color as a diagnostic indicator, ingesting these foods makes an accurate reading impossible.

3. Performing the Medicine Buddha *sadhana* before the visit is also of great benefit. Historically, the patient made a practice of envisioning the doctor as the Medicine Buddha. Traditional doctors perform the ceremony as well. Two minds, it is believed, concentrating on the same healing power increases its effectiveness by a substantial factor.

Preparation on the Day of Consultation

1. Avoid taking a hot shower in the morning, as the subtle channels which carry body energies will be affected. Certain characteristics of the pulse can also be affected.

2. Collect approximately 100 ml of your first morning urine in a clean, transparent glass vessel with a tightly fitting lid. Take the

sample about halfway through the elimination.

3. If your visit is before 10 am, you should probably avoid breakfast, but warm water or weak tea is fine. The key factor to remember is that you should be neither too hungry nor too full. If you are really hungry and have a long wait, then the chances are that this state will be reflected as some type of physical weakness. There may, for example, be signs of low blood pressure in the pulse. This state might lead the doctor to a misdiagnosis.

4. Do not hurry to the appointment, but take your time instead. Try to arrive at least ten minutes early so that you can sit calmly and quietly in the waiting room. In one case, a Tibetan doctor detected the effects of a bumpy fourteen-hour bus ride from Calcutta to Kalimpong even though two days had elapsed since the journey.

5. The consultation should take place as early as possible in the morning, since the pulse will reflect the day's activities. Clients rushing to the clinic at the end of the day will very likely not have an accurate pulse diagnosis.

6. Describe your symptoms specifically. If the Tibetan doctor has had some training in allopathic medicine, a file containing results of allopathic tests and treatment recommendations might be useful. It is important to remember, though, that the diagnostic techniques unique to Tibetan medicine can by themselves bring about excellent results.

7. Studying the basic principles of Tibetan medicine prior to your visit will save you and the doctor time during the interview. If the doctor feels certain that you understand the fundamentals, such

as the concepts of wind, bile, and phlegm, then more time can be devoted to a discussion of the problem itself.

8. Be certain to describe any Western medications you currently take, since this may affect the type, quantity, and time of ingestion of any Tibetan prescription the doctor may recommend. Tibetan medicine, however, can often be combined with other forms of treatment, including alternative techniques such as homeopathy.

9. Taking detailed notes of your consultation will help you and the physician with subsequent visits. Recommendations in dietary and behavioral changes, prescription names, quantities and time of intake are all important factors. Visiting doctors often prescribe a three-month supply of medicine, but whenever possible, a regular check up every two or three weeks is desirable. After even a few days, medication can alter the chemistry in the body.

10. You can recite the Medicine Buddha mantra before taking the pills. According to the practice, medicine is considered as similar to precious jewels. First, offer these jewels to the Buddha and bodhisattvas (enlightened beings). Next, mentally transform these offerings into a life-giving nectar which fills both your body and mind with healing power. This practice can be performed with any type of medicine or even food. As you might expect, there are various versions of this medicine blessing practice, but the principles are the same.

11. Remember that Tibetan doctors are not miracle workers. They are highly trained specialists who, among other things, understand and can detect subtle relationships within your body.

12. The consultation itself should be conducted in an atmosphere conducive to meditation and a relaxed state of mind. The importance of this factor cannot be overstated.

The Eminent Doctor's Excellent Reply

I wanted to learn as much as I could about how Tibetan healing is actually practiced and whether Westerners could benefit from its approach. So, in addition to the interviews I conducted in person during my trip to Nepal and India, I also sought the views of respected Tibetan physicians by mail. The challenge of such interviews is compounded when the questioner and the interview subject do not share a language. Luckily, interested friends were eager to help.

With the help of an associate, I prepared a list of questions for Dr. Sonam Wangdu Changbhar, Gold Medalist in Tibetan Medicine and Honorary Advisor to the Indian Board of Alternative Medicines. We mailed them off to Dr. Changbhar's clinic in Calcutta, and several weeks later I received the eminent doctor's excellent reply.

Peter: Making Tibetan medicine is a process which requires many steps. Blessing the medicine is one of them. Why is this step important?

Dr. Sonam Changbhar: Yes, making Tibetan medicine requires many steps like detoxification, purification, and eliminating the poisonous parts of most of the ingredients. Tibetan physicians do not treat the body as a machine but treat it physically, mentally, and spiritually through the unique system of Tibetan Medical Healing Science and its holistic approach. Therefore, the blessing of medicine is considered to be important.

Peter: Can you outline for us how blessing the medicine is conducted?

Dr. Changbhar: Blessing the medicine is conducted by performing rituals and by reciting the mantras of the Eight Manifestations of Medicine Buddha who have vowed to ease the sufferings of the sick. This helps to purify the medicine spiritually and subsequently to receive blessings from the Medicine Buddhas.

Peter: Can you explain the role of a mantra in blessing or in healing? How exactly does a mantra work?

Dr. Changbhar: According to the Buddhist religion, there are millions of Buddhas and bodhisattvas, as countless as there are dust particles, and each has taken a vow to manifest different capacities for different purposes. When we recite a mantra, we are calling upon that particular Buddha or bodhisattva for help. For instance, for longevity of life, Buddha Amitayus is called upon. For wisdom and knowledge, Manjushri is called upon. For alleviation of sufferings, the Medicine Buddhas are called upon, and so on. In this way, both blessing and healing are accomplished.

Peter: I have seen some healers work simply by passing their

hands over the body of their patient. Have you heard of such things, and do you know how the process works?

Dr. Changbhar: Generally, there are different rituals and practices for different Buddhas and bodhisattvas each having respective powers and subsequent benefits. There are 80,000 obstacles caused by the evil spirits, according to Buddhism, and so there are many rituals for the expulsion of interfering adversities. If the healer is genuine, fully qualified, and specialized in the field, he surely possesses some power, and no doubt, there would be some fruitful result. Conversely, if the healer is not genuine, there would be no benefit.

Peter: People in the West suffer from a number of chronic diseases. One of the most common is headache. They take enormous numbers of pills to relieve the pain, but this only treats the symptoms. Can you suggest some simple measures they might take to treat one of the common causes, which is mental and physical stress?

Dr. Changbhar: Yes, painkillers only kill the pain but not the cause. People in the West lead a very competitive and superficial life, sadly not realizing that as we were born, so must we die someday, whether rich or poor. This lifestyle leads to perpetual anxiety, physical and mental tensions, and stress. Human wants are unlimited, and so people should be content with what they are and with what they possess. This will definitely reduce anxiety and mental tension, which are the major causes of the emergence of common diseases.

Peter: Many people in the Western world realize the benefits of Tibetan medicine. But it will take several generations to train

Westerners in the practice, and even then it may not be possible to transmit the required knowledge. Can you suggest some small but important steps Westerners might take to relieve some of their health problems?

Dr. Changbhar: It is true that the transmission of the required knowledge would not be possible, even after generations. Because to be efficient in Tibetan medicine, one must first learn Tibetan language thoroughly in order to understand the precise medical terminology. The translation of medical terminology is insufficient, even today. For instance, Tibetan medicine is based on the three body humors namely *lung* (wind), *tripa* (bile), and *beygen* (phlegm). But even these translations are inadequate and do not correspond precisely to Tibetan medical terms.

Tibetan medicine operates on three basic principles: diet, proper behavioral patterns, and medication. Diet and behavioral patterns are associated with us daily, and when there is an imbalance in these two, it results in a disease, and we have to turn to medicine for a cure. The imbalance can be corrected by consuming a balanced diet, which forms the basis of good health, by regular exercise, and appropriate behavior. This prevents us from getting diseases.

Peter: Can you discuss the relationship between mind and disease?

Dr. Changbhar: Mind and disease are interrelated. The three body humors are the essential components which regulate all the normal functions of the body and maintain a delicate balance, rendering the individual free of disease. According to the tripod theory of the Three Poisons, the cause of most diseases lies in the mind,

because the body follows the mind.

The Three Poisons—desire, anger, and ignorance—arise out of mind and disturb this delicate balance. The consequences are: desire/attachment leads to *lung* (wind); anger/hatred leads to *tripa* (bile); ignorance/closed-mindedness leads to *beygen* (phlegm). So this unique system treats physically as well as mentally.

Peter: It is said in the texts that the source of all disease is ignorance. What does this mean?

Dr. Changbhar: It is very true that the source of *all* disease and sufferings is ignorance, or our misapprehension of phenomena as being truly existent. In actuality, we are unaware of the real truth—the deep meaning of emptiness. Therefore, we are born into the six realms of cyclic existence (*samsara*). Even if we know we are to die tomorrow, we will be planning many things for our life, because we are influenced by the Three Poisons of human acts due to our ignorance. Unless and until we are enlightened, our minds will be continuously influenced by these three. Therefore, all sufferings are caused by ignorance.

Peter: In recent times, Tibetan doctors have been recruited to go on tours. This means that they travel from city to city, staying only a day or perhaps a week in each place before moving on. In each location, they see a great number of patients. But usually, there isn't enough time for follow-up visits. This means the doctor will not be around in the future to care for his patients. What do you think of this practice?

Dr. Changbhar: It is said that something is better than nothing. Keeping this saying in mind, those who cannot avail themselves of regular visits to a clinic can have a chance to benefit from Tibetan medicine. But certainly, it is very important to follow up the cases, because the patient's life is in the doctor's hands, and doctors should take responsibility for the patient's health. Moreover, Tibetan medicine is a slow process and must be continued for some time to treat chronic diseases.

At the same time, the doctor cannot continue the practice at one place for many months because of visa limitations. Therefore, it would be a lot easier if the WHO [World Health Organization] and the international community recognized and accepted Tibetan medicine officially as an alternative treatment and helped open permanent centers in different cities, so that people could avail themselves of this unique natural system of treatment.

Peter: I went to a Tibetan doctor in the West. He was very thorough, and we got along well. However, after the diagnosis, the doctor prescribed some pills. Then, I got the bill. The secretary charged more than 3000 rupees (approximately $50.00) for a several-week supply of pills. I have heard of other cases where even more is charged. Many people had hoped that Tibetan medicine would become a viable alternative to costly allopathic medicine. But at prices such as these, this medicine, too, will be out of reach of poor people. Can you comment?

Dr. Changbhar: Well, if you ask this question to the doctor himself, he might give you the right answer. I think what you paid is expensive as compared to India. But I understand the huge expenditures a doctor has to bear in traveling to and fro carrying a stock of

medicines from East to West and the high cost of living in the West.

Another important aspect to mention is the high cost of the ingredients of Tibetan medicine and the difficulty in procuring such things as musk, elephant gall stone, and bear bile. Even if ingredients are available, they are very expensive. Saffron costs 50,000 rupees (approximately $1200) for a kilogram. Those medicinal plants which grow above 15,000 feet are very rare and so require special attention. The life of flower herbs is sometimes only a day or a week. Hence, the doctor has to arrive at the right season, right place, and right time to get a particular herb.

Metals, minerals, precious and semiprecious minerals like gold, silver, diamond, sapphire, turquoise, pearl, and coral are also used in some Tibetan precious pills. The poisonous part of the minerals and stones are eliminated by the process of precipitation and are finally burnt to ashes.

In the case of detoxification and precipitation of the mercury used in certain medicines, at least ten people are required to carry out the process for six months. Thus, the making of genuine Tibetan medicine is time-consuming and expensive. The question of genuineness assumes prime importance. Quality control and standardization in terms of the ingredients as well as the finished pills and price control are very important to maintaining good service for patients. There should be some kind of controls, as in Dharamsala, where the Department of Health of the Central Tibetan Administration registers genuinely qualified Tibetan doctors.

Tibetan doctors treat patients kindly and compassionately. Every qualified doctor takes an oath to serve the sufferings of the

people. And in that capacity, doctors can charge fees, depending on the capacity of the patient, providing services totally free for those who cannot afford to pay.

In the eighth century, the Tibetan King Trisong Detsen made it a rule to pay doctors in gold and silver for their services, since doctors are lifesavers. Also, drinking and indecent behavior were strictly prohibited for doctors. These are two of the thirteen rules and regulations imposed by the King.

Peter: Many Western people are learning to make their own medicine, or at least they are trying to make it. There are a number of reasons for this, but the most important is that they want to try to help themselves. Can you make some suggestions as to how they might prepare medicines? What steps might they take to make their medicine more effective?

Dr. Changbhar: I think it is not advisable for people to prepare medicine without thorough knowledge, which can only be obtained by undergoing rigorous training. Identification of the ingredients; their potential, taste, nature, quality, and effects; processes like detoxification, precipitation, and elimination and whether these match accordingly or not must also be known. Even if the potency and nature of ingredients is appropriate, their effects may differ, as the nature of the ingredients is influenced by the five elements (earth, water, fire, air, and space) during their growth. If the composition does not match perfectly, then the result can be adverse or fatal.

Most important, the Tibetan system of medicine remained secret for well over a thousand years. Physicians in Tibet kept it closely guarded. The genuine, specialized, and practical methods remained

as a hereditary profession, its secrets handed over from a father to his son or sometimes from a teacher to a single disciple. After all, it is a matter of precious life and death. Before undertaking any preparations to manufacture medicine, the secret of this unique system of treatment must be known at the grassroots level. Only then can it contribute towards the betterment of mankind.

Peter: Can you offer Westerners some suggestions about taking care of their own health?

Dr. Changbhar: Food forms the basis of good health. So, adopt a proper and balanced diet and regular exercise. Appropriate food habits—neither excess nor deficient—maintain the balance of the three body humors, which helps in proper blood circulation and maintenance of the body organs and channels.

Peter: What do you feel will happen to the Medicine Buddha tradition in the future?

Dr. Changbhar: I am optimistic about the future of the Medicine Buddha tradition. I think with time, this unique system of treatment will be known far and wide and enjoy global recognition and acceptability. And with the blessings of the Medicine Buddhas, less human suffering will prevail.

I am grateful to my son Jigme Namgyal for helping me with my English.

Dr. Changbhar's authoritative response added weight to several convictions I had been forming. Although skeptical by nature, I was becoming thoroughly convinced that the Medicine Buddha healing tradition was, in many ways, a valid and worthy alternative to Western medicine. At the very least, it could supplement our own system, especially in the area of preventive care.

After having met both students and a number of doctors, I also realized that, by any standards, Tibetan medical people were well educated, capable, and trained in a robust and practical tradition. Most importantly, their healing tradition had for centuries cultivated insights into the nature of illness and disease, particularly those related to the mind that Western sciences have only begun to explore.

As I was soon to discover firsthand, the Tibetan healing tradition is not the only successful medical system practiced in the region. I had read of other systems, Unani and Ayurveda, for example, which were even older than the Medicine Buddha tradition. I also had heard of individual traditions which were not rooted in the distant past, but sprang up recently, even within my lifetime.

My time in Nepal was coming to an end. I was eager to make the trip into India and to see these practices for myself.

CHAPTER SEVEN

Journey to Kalimpong

In the heat of the day, I boarded a bus bound for the east, to Kakarbhitta on the Indian border. Buy your ticket in advance, I had been warned, and make sure your seat is near the front. This was good advice, for the old rattletrap was packed—standing room only.

Even though I was seated, the trip was among the most uncomfortable I have ever made. For starters, though I was sitting hunched over, my head hit the luggage rack at every bump. There were many. Then there were the odd colored interior lights, yellow, green, blue, that flickered on and off seemingly at random. The tape player worked in much the same way, sputtering out broken musical phrases every so often.

As for the vehicle's safety, suffice to say that despite the balding tires, we survived the harrowing twelve-hour journey, though we lurched around hairpin turns and swerved wildly to avoid pedestrians and whatever else was on the road. From the window, the faint glow of campfires illuminated little houses scattered throughout the countryside. Who were these people, I wondered? What were their hopes and ambitions?

Watching the driver was the most interesting event of the ride. He had no fewer than nine assistants packed into his cab, their shoulders huddled together, their eyes glued to the road. What they were looking for so intently, I never did find out. With the guidance of this committee, we sped our way through a long, tortuous night, arriving at the

border station sometime before breakfast.

Kakarbhitta was the first jungle I had ever seen. While waiting for the border official to shave and dress, I watched the morning scene unfold along the river. Water buffaloes herded by youthful masters ambled peacefully along in the shallows. Fishermen stood patiently by the bank. Families frolicked and bathed in midstream. Every now and then, the low, dim hum of the background hustle and bustle was pierced by the sharp cry of some exotic bird.

Behind me, on the bridge, the day's traffic began in earnest. The women carried their wares, while the men peddled their rickshaws, some carrying passengers, some on the prowl for fares. The bridge was quite new, but the rest of the town had seemingly not changed in a thousand years. There was a rhythm here, a pace of life that I somehow understood. Mother India! Soon enough, I found myself in the rear of a jeep, also packed with luggage and passengers.

Once again we recklessly threaded our way along narrow roads through the West Bengal hills toward Kalimpong. Here I had arranged to meet Barbara Gerke, founder of the International Trust for Traditional Medicine (ITTM), and her associates. Or so I had thought. As it turned out, she did not receive the fax I had sent her from Katmandu several weeks earlier until I handed it to her in person. When I arrived in town, this same fax was handed to me when I inquired about directions to the ITTM. No one, it seems had been walking in that direction recently, and so it had not been delivered—a hopelessly inefficient system, but endearing nonetheless.

Like most places in the West Bengal Hills, Kalimpong is built on the side of a hill of monumental proportions. These "hills" range between 5,000 and 10,000 feet high. This geography makes walking a superb form of exercise.

Over the next month, I spent my days meeting a bewildering array of healers from many traditions. Barbara Gerke made sure of it!

A WIDE RANGE OF LOCAL PRACTICES

It does not take a visitor to Kalimpong very long to realize that many systems of medicine are practiced here. It is not uncommon to see signs which point to clinics for Unani, Tibetan, homeopathic, and Ayurvedic practices. These larger, well-known systems seem to coexist peacefully. But there are other healing traditions as well. Some are young, having existed for only a few generations; others date back centuries.

The Nepali and Lepcha people who live in the Bengal Hills, for example, each have very effective and ancient traditions of healing. Unlike Tibetan methods, these systems rely on simple remedies, such as mixing a plant with water to form a blood-clotting paste. These healing practices can be very effective in on-the-spot emergencies, but immediate applications seem to be the extent of their usefulness.

Confronted by this wide range of methods and by their obvious usefulness to the local population, I decided to broaden my initial focus on distinctly Tibetan ideas about medicine. Using the resources of the ITTM, I determined to explore as many traditions as possible during my stay. It was a wise decision, for I met many fascinating healers, each with specialized knowledge and a unique world view. Locating Tibetan healing within this wider context helped me appreciate its finer qualities.

As the founder of the International Trust for Traditional Medicine, Barbara Gerke's responsibilities are numerous. She not only facilitates the visits and research programs of visiting scholars, but works closely with many of the local people. Pictured here with Geeta Sharma, Barbara has also developed several programs for children in the neighborhood.

THE HEALERS

The Lepcha Healer

The Lepchas are the indigenous people of a large region which includes Kalimpong. They call their medicine "Joo" therapy. It depends heavily on animal derivatives such as deer liver and various parts of others animals such as the fox and jackal. Many of these animals are now very rare, and the government has rightly banned their killing. As a consequence, the Lepchas have turned outside their own community for healing.

The chapel at the leper colony in Kalimpong. The victims here were well cared for and, considering their plight, seemed peaceful and comfortable. Elsewhere, on the streets of the major cities and in tourist towns, for example, many others were not so fortunate.

Some old-timers, though, still practice Joo therapy. I was told about one Lepcha healer, Ong Tshering, who is well known internationally. Even though I did not meet him personally, I was very impressed by reports of his skill and compassion. Reputed to be more than ninety years old, Ong Tshering is unique for a number of reasons. In the first place, he refuses payment for his work. In the second, he does not charge room and board if the patient must remain in his clinic. For Ong Tshering, I came to understand, healing is not a business; it is a service.

Ong Tshering lives alone on his vast property in the district of Darjeeling. When patients seek his help, he welcomes them. Some of his healings are reported to be instantaneous. In true Lepcha tradition, he uses the strangest

ingredients, such as the nails of birds and the bones of animals to perform his "miracles."

Over the years, Ong Tshering has become very well known. His clients include eminent politicians and the very wealthy, who travel long distances from Rajanistan, Delhi, Bombay, and Calcutta to seek his advice and ask for his healing.

The Mataji Kumari Cintury

The Mataji Kumari Cintury is a well-known healer in the bustling, prosperous city of Darjeeling. She is the priestess of a temple located near the downtown core. Together with Barbara and several friends, I had the good fortune to spend two afternoons with her. We discussed many aspects of her healing art. On the last afternoon, she performed divinations for each of us, admitted us to her innermost shrine, and left us with her blessings.

The Mataji had been ill for some time and was just beginning to recover when she granted our audience. Despite her obvious discomfort, she displayed a warm and loving nature. She revealed something of her relationship to her spiritual mentor, whom she called the Devi and identifies with the Hindu goddess Durga, the feminine representation of primordial universal energy.

The Mataji Kumari Cintury. The term Mataji literally means "Dear Mother." Spirituality, she said, can best be achieved through service and devotion to the poor, the weak, and the sick. Her practical contribution to service is building a home for destitute children and growing medicinal plants in soil purified by her prayers.

How The Mataji Kumari Cintury Became a Healer

The Mataji told us many stories, including an account of her discovery of her connection with the Devi, the source of her healing power and wisdom. The story begins when she is a child in a Darjeeling elementary school.

After a lengthy illness, Mataji returned to school to find that she had a strange ability. She found that by swallowing her study notes, she would instantly have complete recall of whatever was written down. One day, the classroom teacher caught her and was understandably upset. As Mataji tells it:

". . . so she [the teacher] lost her temper and gave me a good, solid beating. This happened more than once. One day, after the beating, I fell into a trance and removed all of my clothes except my undergarments and placed them before the teacher.

"Not knowing what I was doing, I walked out nearly naked to a small hill called Mahakal [the Darjeeling Observatory Hill] and sat there in a trance. Nobody was there. All of the students, apart from me, had returned home, and people were looking for me. While I was sitting there, somebody pushed me to wake me up, though nobody was around. But the push took me out of the trance and, after that, I walked home.

"Soon after that, I had a dream. One of the Hindu gods, Ganesha, the god of wisdom and wealth [with the elephant head], appeared

in front of me with two beautiful books, one wrapped in white, and one in red. He asked me: 'Which one do you want?' I chose the red one. When I took it, Ganesha said: 'Since you have selected the red book, there is no need for you to acquire any outside knowledge. You need not go in for any external studies.' At that time, I was in class seven, and I stopped going to school.

"Every evening I would light a candle and then go out to play. When I felt the shivering sensations up my spine, I would go home and rest. This is how the years passed.

"I slowly realized that the Devi was all-pervasive inside me. In my dreams I was exposed to the most holy Hindu scripture—the *Chandi*. There would be times when the Devi would take me along physically, to teach me—at times to the jungle, at times to the forests. Thrice I was taken to a remote cave in the forest for meditation. Then I could perceive the shadow of the Devi. I did not have a guru as such. All knowledge was given to me by the Devi. All my mantras came to me from the Devi. Since then I have felt the presence of the Devi all the time, even now. That is how I became the Mataji."

We asked Mataji to speak about the practice of blessing the medicine, her formulas for curing diseases, the effects of magic, and the importance of service to others.

"Nowadays," she told us, "there is no culture to bless the medicine in the Western tradition. This culture should be developed. Blessing medicines adds to their healing power and is of benefit for the people being healed. The medicines I prepare are for particular diseases. Heal-

ing knowledge is given to me by the Devi. She tells me how to prepare them from plants and barks. That medicine is invariably blessed by Her.

"Having the ill person in mind, I also recite a mantra. Then the medicine is applied. Everyone who has been treated by this blessed medicine has been cured or has improved considerably. The patient's belief in both the cure and the medicine is important for the effect."

Mataji then asked her assistant to bring out a wooden box from a nearby cabinet. From it she took a number of bottles, each filled with a different colored substance.

"This is a powdered medicine that is prepared for serious cases of sinus. It is blessed with my Rudraksha rosary. This is not an ordinary rosary. You can buy similar beads in the market, but these beads were given to me by the Devi. She told me to go to a forest and pick the seeds from a particular tree. The beads are inside a shell which has to be removed. I collected them and prepared this rosary.

"My work is not miraculous. Success depends on the severity of the illness. If cancer patients come in a terminal stage, they cannot be cured. But in the early stages, it is possible. I have successfully treated such patients. Epilepsy and tuberculosis can be also treated. The medicine for tuberculosis is grown underground. This makes it difficult, because some people avoid medicines grown in such places.

The representation of Durga found in the Mataji Kumari Cintury's shrine in Darjeeling.

"When you cure illness or worry, you take

the problem and absorb it within yourself. You might think that this is a burden, but it is not. I have to meditate and recite mantras continuously. Only then am I able to do these things. If I increase someone's life span by one element, I must give that same element from my own life. But I do not think about this. It is up to the Devi to decide. We live for others. Our own life does not really matter."

The Mataji uses her abilities for many purposes including combating evil spells. She told us that in India, even today, many diseases are caused by dark forces. Some people pay black magicians to bring misfortune and illness to a certain person. This effect is possible if the practitioner is given some hair, nails, or a piece of cloth belonging to the person.

"I am able to detect if black magic is involved in an illness," the Mataji told us, "and neutralize it through mantras and prayers. The source of the black magic evoked is mostly the dark side of goddess Kali. I have been given a special mantra to protect myself while I work against the magic spells, because in the past [evil forces] have directed their attack against me. For a whole day and night I have to recite a mantra for protection before counteracting the spell."

We left the Mataji with our good wishes and our hopes that we would one day meet again.

The Amazing Bone Healer

Sixteen miles from the River Teesta, between Kalimpong and Lava, is the clinic of "The Amazing Bone Healer," Mr. Baidhya Chhewang Pakhrin. The twenty-bed clinic was constructed in 1995 entirely through donations and public contributions. It sits beside the main road, perched precariously on a cliff.

Mr. Pakhrin's gift of restoring broken bones is acknowledged by people from all walks of life: politicians, medical doctors, the middle

class, as well as the poor and helpless. People from all over India seek him out. In fact, they come from as far away as Bhutan and Nepal. During both of my visits, his institute was full. In fact, it is always busy. According to one report, during forty years of practice, The Amazing Bone Healer has successfully treated more than thirty thousand patients. As the years roll by, he becomes busier still.

Although his reputation is largely built upon his success mending broken bones, he also treats sciatica, arthritis, gout, rheumatism, spondylitus (inflammation of the spinal column), hemorrhoids, urinary tract infections, and genital diseases. While he has studied Unani medicine, Mr. Pakhrin is not trained as an allopathic doctor. Rather, he claims that his special healing knowledge was given to him in dreams by a holy man. He is not the first in his family to have been granted this information, as he carries on a healing tradition kept in the family for five generations. Now, he says, his dream teacher appears to his daughter as well.

The first dream came to his great-grandfather, a hunter in the jungles of Nepal. One night, on an overnight campout, Mr. Pakhrin's ancestor saw something eerie, the head of a tiger appearing among the foliage of a large creeper nearby. Others present saw nothing. The next day, the group killed a deer, which they cut into pieces and wrapped in leaves from the same creeper where the tiger had appeared. Later, when the meat was unwrapped, the hunters discovered that the individual pieces had fused together!

That night, the hunter had a dream in which a holy man appeared. In the dream, the holy man gave him knowledge of both herbal medicine and healing mantras. From that time, certain members of the Pakhrin family have been healers. They have made it a policy to work solely for the good of the poor and sick and never for profit.

The Miraculous Bone Healer. For four generations, Mr. Pakhrin's family has held the secret of restoring broken bones. When he retires, his daughter will continue the tradition. His thriving clinic is a fine testament to the efficacy of the techniques he uses.

I asked Mr. Pakhrin about his practice and whether others could learn it. After long consideration, he said, "Remember, this art is not easily learned." He continued by saying that he might take some students, if they were suitable, but so far, very few candidates have had the patience. His daughter, he added, and three assistants who have been with him for nineteen years now, were exceptions.

He spoke of the personal qualities of students: "They must be honest, pure, religious, with a genuine wish to serve. I cannot give this art to those who wish to profit from it. Greed can destroy this gift. And that is why this knowledge has to be bestowed in safe hands."

Rather than charging for his services, Mr. Pakhrin accepts whatever donations his patients can afford, and he allows them to stay in his clinic as long as necessary for their recovery. Often a family member cares for the patient during the stay. When I mentioned that an overnight stay in a Western hospital might cost 20,000 rupees (roughly $525), he became serious and said, "a few hundred rupees [$5 to $10] would do here."

"The art of healing is a gift from God to mitigate the sufferings of the people," he continued. "This is not for money and that is why I make no charges. The people give what they can. It is they who keep the place running. There is no government funding, although I admit pleading for it several times in the past. Instead of receiving money, I had to confront several hindrances. Some accused me of secretly practicing allopathic medicines under the guise of Ayurveda. They searched the whole place for evidence. They tried to destroy my reputation. But they failed. They found nothing that proved their charges. Thankfully, concerned authorities issued me a certificate on the credibility of my medicine, and I circulated it to the doctors who had tried to malign me."

Mr. Pakhrin now requires all patients to bring X-rays of their broken bones before he admits them to his care. He uses these for diagnostic purposes. His medications are largely herbal, derived from plants in the forest. He prefers herbs, he says, to pharmaceutical drugs. While

both forms of medicine can heal deeply, prescription drugs, he maintains, often have damaging side effects, while herbs do not.

As for the principles of healing, he claims that his are the same as those in the allopathic tradition. He explained something of his art: "The first thing I do is hypnotize the person. Patients must have confidence in me. Then, if you set the bones properly, they will heal naturally. Apply a medicinal paste together with a bamboo splint, and this holds the bones firmly. In [Western] orthopedics lies a fault. The plaster of Paris cast shrinks as it dries, leaving room for the bones to play. Sometimes the plaster dries more quickly on the side exposed to the air. This, too, causes problems. Using bamboo splints instead reduces that risk."

When I asked him about the future, Mr. Pakhrin told me that he sincerely hoped that his style of practice would become established in centers far from his clinic—in Sikkim, Darjeeling, and Siliguri. During the tour of his clinic, I spoke with his patients and looked at their X-rays. Family members mingled freely, and everyone seemed truly grateful for this bone doctor. Some who were recovering sat outside in the warmth of the sun. Others lay on their cots. All felt fortunate that they had found their way to Mr. Pakhrin's clinic.

Though he did not disclose which ones, Mr. Pakhrin did say that he regularly collects fresh medicinal plants which he makes into pastes and decoctions for the treatment of broken bones.

The Amazing Bone Healer's Eight Keys to Success

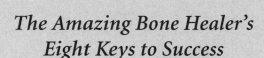

● Fresh medical plants are collected regularly from forests and private farms.

● These are dried, compounded, and made into pastes, dusts, and decoctions as they are required.

● Patients are questioned, and if X-rays are required, they are sent to other clinics. Otherwise, they are free to remain as long as the treatment takes.

● A local anesthetic, made from nine ingredients, is applied.

● The bone is set, using an herbal paste, and is framed in bamboo splints. This frame is carefully tightened by plastering techniques.

● Fifteen days of bed rest are advised, after which the frame is undone and the bone examined.

● New herbal medicines are applied, the frame is reset, and another fifteen days of bed rest recommended.

● After thirty days, the frame is removed. In successful cases, the patient leaves the clinic two to four weeks later.

NARPRASAD GURUNG AND THE FIELD TRIP TO LAVA

Day after day, O.B. Dass took me on extensive walking tours. Our mission was to meet and interview every healer in Kalimpong. Tireless and persistent, even though he was 15 years my senior, he wore me completely out after just a few short weeks. My mentor and friend, I salute him now in all his endeavors.

Most of my time so far had been taken up tromping around the crowded areas of cities and towns. So it was with great relief that I accepted my friend O. B. Dass's invitation to hike through the forested hills to Lava, a small village at the edge of the Himalayas. On the way, we would seek out and discuss the history and therapeutic properties of as many medical plants as possible.

O. B. Dass had a surprise for me. His associate, Narprasad Gurung, an herbalist living in one of the outlying settlements, would accompany us. We had only to hike along a woodland trail to his small farm in the interior. Then he would guide us, explaining what he knew of the therapeutic properties of the plants we encountered.

The trailhead began at an elevation of 7,300 feet. From that height, we proceeded upward, eventually arriving at the village of Lava. In my part of the world, such an elevation assures the presence of snow at almost any time of the year. Here, however, no snow ever falls. This meant that the forest we walked through was magnificent. Plants of all sizes and descriptions were growing everywhere in lush profusion.

Not so long ago, O. B. Dass told me, orchids graced the forest canopy in prodigious numbers. Unfortunately for the orchid population, however, plant lovers the world over found out how beautiful they are. With the increase in demand, exporters hired local villagers to collect specimens.

Wild plants were shipped to the four corners of the earth. The "pickers," as they were called, were relentless in their pursuit and would climb even the tallest trees seeking these spectacular parasites in their most secret refuge.

But the picker's heyday had come and gone. In an attempt to protect the remaining plants, the Indian government passed a law forbidding the export of wild orchids. Only hybrids grown in nurseries can now be shipped. Despite this action, orchids are somewhat rare. Given sufficient protection, perhaps they will return once again. There is hope. The region has developed a thriving orchid nursery business, and the forests are no longer ruthlessly pillaged for these lovely plants.

The demise of the orchid population underscores a problem with specimen collecting in particular and with Tibetan medicine in general. The combined factors of destroyed habitat and increased demand for medicinal Himalayan plants is threatening many species. Each year the demand for these plants increases. Further, every year a number of new Tibetan doctors graduate from the two main schools in Dharamsala and Lhasa. All of these doctors will require medicine.

Dr. Dawa, the doctor who was one of my teachers back in Ithaca, was certainly aware of the ecological threat. He resolved it in the following way. "All that we see," he said in a lecture, "has medicinal value. But in the future, precious gemstones and animal products will become rare and very expensive. Therefore medicinal plants should be used, because they are found everywhere. They are easily grown and have medicinal value." Though Dr. Dawa's words sounded encouraging, I knew with dramatic certainty that unless humankind attended to the problem, natural forests such as the one I was walking through would soon disappear and, with them, the world's supply of medicinal plants.

The one bright ray of hope is the genuine love many people feel towards living things. While it may not be possible to halt environmental destruction right now, it is possible to preserve many species of plants

and even animals in private sanctuaries until they can be reintroduced into whatever wilderness is set aside. This is the case with orchids. Quite soon many varieties will exist only in private collections.

The Village in the Hills

At the summit of the hill, somewhere in the neighborhood of 8,500 feet, we came upon a group of young men, resting, laughing, and talking. Each of them carried a large basket made of woven reeds. These baskets, now empty, had carried produce from their terraced hillside farms to a drop-off station near the main road. From there, the vegetables would be transported by truck to the market in town. Their hike, repeated every day or so, was roughly fifteen miles.

These young men were more than happy to accompany us to Narprasad's farm. We walked the last four miles in their company.

After some conversation, these young men decided to accompany us, since we were going in the same direction. They were great company, being not only curious about us but happy to discuss their own business. Four miles further, always moving deeper into the forest, the trail opened out onto pasture, and our little band looked down several hundred feet at a little village. Several houses were clustered together, surrounded by the most beautiful terraced gardens imaginable. When we descended, Narprasad Gurung met us and took us into his house. His wife offered us tea and cookies and a welcome break from the heat in the comfort and shade of their tiny house with its breathtaking views.

Villages and settlements such as Narprasad's are common in this area. Most have little communication with the outside world. Even the foot-

path we were using was only a year old. Solid as it looked, it could not be used in the rainy season because of running water, mud, and leeches!

The people in Narprasad's village are Gurkhas who arrived with the British well over a century ago. Originally from Nepal, the men were part of the British army. Their reputation as implacable fighters is, even today, well deserved. Their fame stems, in part, from their use of the razor sharp Kukri, a long-bladed knife with universally respected cutting properties. Even today, the Gurkhas form important brigades in the British, Indian, and Nepalese armies. Their war cry, *"Aayo Gorkhali,"* means, "The Gurkhas are upon you."

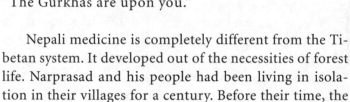

Plants have many uses; this fern, for example, was used as a pen.

Nepali medicine is completely different from the Tibetan system. It developed out of the necessities of forest life. Narprasad and his people had been living in isolation in their villages for a century. Before their time, the Lepchas, the aboriginal inhabitants of the area, lived in this valley. The two groups fought a territorial war in the nineteenth century, which, according to local sources, was won by the Gurkhas. At any rate, the Lepchas were gone, and the Gurkhas remained.

Soon we were on our way, with Narprasad insisting on carrying my small pack. It took quite a while to leave his property, not because it was so vast, but simply because there were so many plants to see and discuss. In fact, the entire afternoon was passed in walking a little and then pausing to investigate a botanical specimen. My two companions scrutinized each variety and then translated their comments for me.

It was obvious that Narprasad was intimately familiar with the botany of the area. Like other members of his settlement, he had grown up using various plants for all kinds of purposes. We came upon a certain fern, for example, which in the past had been used as a writing implement. Shoots cut from the base were used as pens, while ink was

made from the leaves of a bean plant.

By late afternoon Narprasad left us, and O. B. Dass and I continued our walk along a rugged forest path. The trail led through the hills to the forest service station in Lava several kilometers distant. As we walked, my friend explained the importance of traditional healing to the people who lived here and why a thorough knowledge of local herbs was so vital to their welfare. The main thing to realize, he said, was that it was not a simple matter to take a person to town for medical treatment. He asked me to guess how local people were transported to the hospital in emergencies.

Himalayan outpost settlements have little communication with the outside world.

I mentally summarized the facts. Some of the settlements were comprised of only one household. In these tiny outposts, medical problems of any description were obviously a serious problem. Distance and time were factors. The scanty resources of the region, I reasoned, would certainly rule out a helicopter airlift. Jeeps could not navigate these trails. The people did not have horses or even yaks. Try as I might, I could not solve the puzzle. Finally, I gave up.

Smiling at my bafflement, O. B. Dass told me that seriously ill people were bundled into empty gunny sacks. These were then carried on the backs of friends or family members, sometimes many miles, to the nearest road. Many people died on the trail. Villagers knew that if their injuries were too severe, they would not survive such a journey and had to be treated at home. Consequently, they took their medicine very seriously and had local remedies for even the most severe problems.

Medicinal Plant Count

As we worked our way home, the list I was compiling of helpful plants lengthened with each bend in the road. The names of some plants

were given only in Nepali, but for many others, O. B. Dass had an English and even a Latin equivalent.

There was, for example, the *paris plant* whose root is used to counter stomach pains and wounds. The tuberous root of the *pahundid* is used as medicine for blood dysentery, cuts, deep wounds, and diabetes. It is made into a tea and mixed with honey or applied as a paste. Sometimes, the tuber is simply chewed. The milk sap of the *acklebis* is used for boils. We found a *lycopodium* which had both ornamental and medical uses. This plant, said O. B. Dass conclusively, had gunpowder in its spots and was actively hunted by agents for pharmaceutical companies.

Several plants were used against malaria, and another made a fish-killing poison—a useful drug for fishermen. One strange-looking plant was an effective repellent for leeches. It also aided in setting bones. We found plants to combat jaundice, cure animal diseases, and others that were deadly poisons. One specimen was reputed to be an intoxicant to bears, who actively sought it out. Eventually, I got the

We also came upon a variety of rhododendron, the flower of which is said to have many therapeutic uses. Apparently it is effective against blood dysentery and diabetes. Curiously, it is also used to dissolve fish bones stuck in the throat. So widespread is the belief in this extraordinary power that a local saying has sprung up around it: "if a fish bone is stuck in your throat," it says, "just name this flower 'Guras,' and the fish bone goes."

impression that the list of healing or helpful plants was essentially endless.

On another day, our group returned to Lava. Taking chairs from a nearby restaurant, Narprasad, O. B. Dass, Barbara Gerke, and I sat outside on the street discussing medicinal plants. Every passerby seemed irresistibly attracted to our conversation and stopped to listen. One elderly herbalist pulled out his special snake-repelling paste. It worked, he said, not only to prevent poisonous snakes from biting but to keep such snakes completely away—powerful medicine indeed.

The author, Narprasad, O.B. Dass, and bystanders in an animated discussion about herbs and snake-repelling paste.

Soon everyone clamored around him insisting on a little piece. He couldn't escape, and so, with a funny expression on his face, he proceeded to dole it out. I smuggled some home between the pages on my notebook, another artifact for my eccentric museum of curiosities.

After a while, the crowd around us grew so large it attracted the attention of a local official. Bustling over, he demanded to know what was happening. Realizing that we were harmless, he insisted that we join him for tea, where we discussed, among other things, our countries of origin, our purpose in visiting Lava, regional politics, the current state of affairs in the world, and whether or not we liked the tea. He then insisted that should we ever return, we would be his overnight guests.

At day's end, O. B. Dass and I stood alone together on a high point, overlooking a wondrous valley. As the sun set behind the high peaks in the west, we stood trying to decide the name of an odd

looking parasitic plant clinging to the side of a dead tree. Just above it hung a cluster of white orchids in full bloom. Our voices assumed a quiet, almost reverential tone in the early twilight. Only the sound of the cuckoo birds broke the silence, their peculiar calls melding well with the long evening shadows. As the hush of true dusk dropped like a canopy over the forest, even the cuckoos fell silent.

NATURE'S PHARMACY

Mongol doctors, it is said, use every conceivable plant to make medicines. A story is told about a doctor teacher who sent his students into the forest during an examination with instructions to collect those plants which cannot be used in medicine. All the students returned with multiple specimens, except for one young man who returned empty handed, saying that there is nothing in the forest without medicinal value. That student was given the full mark and, later on, became a famous doctor.

One afternoon at the ITTM in Kalimpong, Professor Lama Chimpa, a Mongolian himself, reinforced my impression that nature is a fully stocked pharmacy. "Medicines," he told me, "are made from all sorts of materials. Some physicians practice only water treatment. Such a doctor collects water from various sources: from the sea, from the top of a mountain stream, from wells, dewdrops, rain water, melted snow. All of these samples are kept in different containers for months or years at appropriate temperatures. Some of this water is boiled, while some is kept in the sun. There are people who have blind faith in water treatment. It is said the water treatments are very good in acidic trouble or stomach upsets.

"No part of the plant is left unused in medical compounds. The roots, sap, flowers, and leaves are all used in medicine preparation. Not a single flower is considered useless for medical composition.

"Once I heard a Mongol doctor say that all of those flowers on which

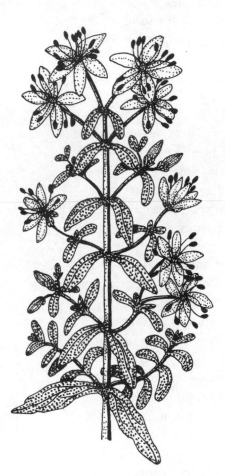

butterflies sit are ready medicine for various diseases. And these offer good vitamins, too. One can eat such flowers without any hesitation. A flower rejected by butterflies is poison. But even if it is poisonous, it becomes medicine when it is properly composed. Like a notorious thief who can become a good and useful person when he is properly trained and taught, a poisonous plant can become very effective medicine. In fact, Mongol and Tibetan doctors use medicines prepared from poisonous plants when the disease is a severe one."

Having seen for myself the riches of nature's medicine cabinet, I readily agreed.

COMMON FOOD PLANTS AND THEIR MEDICINAL PROPERTIES

We typically forget that many common foods have medicinal value. Some of these plants require processing for long-term storage. Others, like barley, beans, garlic, and squashes, can be kept just as they are. These herbs and foods can bring relief for mild headaches, colds, light fevers, minor cuts, and blemishes.

Common wild plants, such as the dandelion, plantain, and sorrel are very powerful herbs. The dandelion, for example, is unparalleled in stimulating the flow of bile from the liver. St. John's Wort, currently hailed as an effective, natural antidepressant, is sold in grocery stores throughout the world at very high prices. The plant, as it turns out, has a long history of medicinal use and has

St. John's Wort, currently popular in the United States and Europe as an alternative antidepressant, has a long history of medicinal use.

always been well known for its therapeutic properties. It grows everywhere and spreads rapidly. Interestingly, it is classified as an undesirable weed in Idaho and everywhere else there is grazing land. By 1950, this plant, a native of Europe, had, as the Forest Service put it, "infested" approximately 600,000 acres of land. Poison to one is manna to another.

Common Food Plants and their Medicinal Properties

PLANT	MEDICINAL PROPERTY
apples	a mild laxative
asparagus	diuretic
barley	demulcent
basil	antispasmodic
beans	diuretic
garlic	anthelmintic (vermifuge)
ginger	diaphoretic
onion	antiseptic and tonic
orange	carminative
soy beans	natural source of estrogen

CHAPTER EIGHT

Healing Sounds and Symbols

I n the early hours of the morning, I awoke to a strange sound echoing through the Bengal Hills. It was haunting, something like the call of a cow moose in rut. I lay awake for a long time, thinking, probing my memory. Then I had it. The sound was made by a conch shell trumpet. Such horns had been used in the past by Hawaiians to communicate over long distances, but I had no idea how they were used here. The person on the other end of the conch, I reasoned, must be trying to contact someone—but who and where?

I fell to sleep again, lulled by the distant droning. Later that morning, I told Lama Chimpa about the exciting sounds I had heard. There's no mystery, he told me. Conch shell trumpets are used in *pujas*, ceremonies which make offerings to the Buddhas and other protective beings.

One of the most striking features among both Tibetan lamas and the other traditional healers I had met was the variety of spiritual equipment they used to induce healing effects. These included spectacular paintings, sculpted images, trumpets and horns, rosaries, bells, prayer flags—symbols of every conceivable size and shape, for every conceivable purpose.

As I thought about these devices, I realized that using them amounted to communicating in a special language, one that speaks

through abstract symbols engraved on ritual objects, sequences of sound and instruments to make them, ritual gestures, prayers, mythology, poetry, and more. Other methods used by many healers were even more esoteric, including special states of mind cultivated through meditation which are largely invisible to the casual observer.

Over the centuries, these techniques have been refined until, on the surface at least, they appear to be primarily artistic endeavors. In fact, Tibetans have become almost as well known for their skills as artisans as for their spiritual accomplishments. Still, the central purpose of their arts is to aid seekers in their quest for spiritual development.

Conch shell trumpets are easily made. Remove the top inch or so from the spiral tip of the shell. On the inside, you will now be able to see a thin spiraling wall. Scrape this away, and the instrument is ready. Blow it as you would a trumpet, but be prepared for the extraordinary volume of the sound.

INSTRUMENTS OF SOUND

Singing Bowl

Some of the most interesting Tibetan sound-making devices are singing bowls. They are said to "sing" because of the quality of sound they produce when struck or rubbed. Although singing bowls have a long history, it is unclear exactly how the art of making and using them came into being. Most likely, the bowls were developed by shamans who used them in their practice of magic, ritual, and healing.

These bowls have appeared at various times in other cultures. One famous bowl, known as the Chinese fountain bowl, is systematically riddled with small indentations. When filled with water and rubbed in a special way, it produces particular vibrations which cause a fountain

of water to rise. A similar effect, though not nearly so pronounced, will occur when a singing bowl is filled with water and the lip is rubbed in a circular manner with a wooden stick. A crystal glass filled with water and rubbed with a finger will do the same thing, producing sound as well.

Historically, singing bowls have been made from several different metals, each one corresponding to a particular planet. Gold was allied with the Sun, silver with the Moon, mercury with Mercury, copper with Venus, iron with Mars, tin with Jupiter, and lead with Saturn. So, in a sense, singing bowls represent the marriage between aspects of both astrology and alchemy.

It is not difficult to feel the vibrations produced by a bowl. Indeed, when struck, the larger bowls and especially the giant gongs demand your attention. The vibrations seem to stimulate every molecule in your body. There are many theories about the effects of these sounds. Some authorities believe these sounds activate psychophysiological processes in the body which can produce, among other things, healing effects.

How these healings take place is still not understood, since, in the West at least, healing through sound is still an infant science. But it is clear that sound vibrations pass through air and then through the human body. This means that sound vibrations do have a physiological effect. It follows logically that the tones of various instruments can influence aspects of the mind and body.

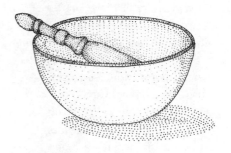

One thing that is certain is that the quality of sound produced by singing bowls lends itself very well to the induction of hypnotic states. These states are well known for their therapeutic effects, especially in promoting relaxation and positive states of mind.

Singing bowls can induce hypnotic states which promote relaxation and positive states of mind.

The Drum

Shamanic practices often use drums as a means of healing and for journeying to other realms of consciousness or even other worlds. Tibetan lamas also use drums to good effect. It is well known that the sound of the drum is used as a means to alter consciousness.

I have participated in drum dances in which an entire community dances together in a great circle, often around the drum itself, or around a stove or open fire. It was clear to me that, during the dance, participants moved out of an everyday state of awareness. For one thing, long-standing feuds were forgotten, temporarily at least, and everyone entered into the magic circle.

Tingshaws

I nstruments are used during ritual and prayer ceremonies of all types, including those devoted to healing. Drums such as this one are common in Tibetan monasteries and are often accompanied by other instruments, such as horns and cymbals. One evening, I stood outside a monastery in Bodhnath for an hour or more as several drum and horn players made their hypnotic music. Darkness fell, and still I was reluctant to leave, the strange sounds having worked their trance-inducing charm.

Tingshaws are small, hand-held cymbals used in ritual. Although they have many uses, one of the most unusual is the practice of "feeding the hungry ghosts." As I described in Chapter 1, the realm of the hungry ghosts is one of the six worlds of samsara, the cycle of reincarnations driven by karma. The spirits of this domain are classified into two groups. Those of the inner realm harm no one; rather, they themselves suffer constantly from insatiable appetites.

The other group of spirits, known as "demons from the outer realm," are habitually malevolent. These beings are believed to cause grief, hardship, and disease, often psychological in nature, wherever they roam. They are also held responsible for some natural disasters, such as hail storms, floods, fires, and so on.

Such dangers to humanity are possible because of our relationship to the five elements. We have seen that Tibetan philosophy links the inner world of body processes to the outer surrounding environment, since both inner and outer worlds are composed of the same five elements. We have also learned that elements inside the body can be unbalanced by afflicted thoughts and emotions. When this happens, corresponding imbalances from the external environment—demons, perhaps—may be attracted. This attraction can manifest as a neurosis or even as a more severe problem such as schizophrenia. These same entities can also afflict an entire community. In these cases, the results may be large-scale disasters, such as hurricanes, floods, earthquakes, or even plagues.

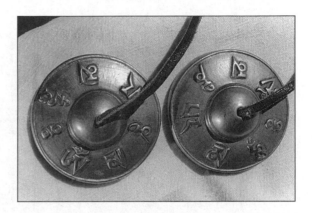

Sound can be used to appease these malevolent spirits as well. Special community ceremonies are held to dispel such "evil" influences. Drums are beaten and horns sounded so as to involve the entire community in the clearing and healing. Tibetan practice in this regard is similar to Native American drum dances in which the entire community participates. I have taken part in several such ceremonies and have seen how they can powerfully rejuvenate the community ethos.

Even if we do not accept the notion of ghosts or demons as actual entities, we can still interpret the "attacks of spirits" as physical manifestations of our negative thoughts and improper actions. Seen in this way, it is our own unexamined mind which is responsible

Once I noticed tingshaws on the lid of a toilet in the washroom of a lamas' house. Naturally, I inquired as to what this wonderful instrument was doing in a privy. "Why, we use them to feed the hungry ghosts," I was told, as if it was perfectly self-evident. "The sound helps to satisfy their craving and eases their suffering." Later, I found out that these ghosts are believed to be attracted to such places. Producing certain sounds is considered both an act of compassion and a means of healing, since it relieves these unfortunate beings of their horrific appetites, temporarily at least.

for the trouble-causing "demons."

Another insight about demons comes from Machig Lapdron, a yogini who lived from 1055-1149. She understood "demons" to be any-thing—even friends and family—whose actions interfered with our own liberation. Greatest among the demons, she said, was the belief in an eternal, imperishable self!

Healing Sounds

You do not need to go to a monastery to experience the effects of healing sounds for yourself. All you need is an instrument, preferably one which makes a clear tone, and a quiet room. If you do not have a singing bowl, tingshaws, or a conch shell trumpet, you might use a crystal goblet.

Pour some water into the goblet, wet your finger, and run it around the rim. Different volumes of water produce different sounds. Experiment with the tones until you find one you especially like. Sound penetrates the body through the ears but also, more directly, through the skin itself. Most people can easily feel these vibrations as a tingling sensation in the palms of their hands. If you feel a little uncomfortable with the novelty of the exercise, relax. People have been using healing sounds for centuries.

Bell and Dorje

The hand bell and five-pronged scepter known as the *dorje* are, per-haps, the most important ritual objects in Tibetan Buddhist practice. They are used by lamas, as I had observed in Ithaca, in every initiation ceremony. They are also used, I discovered, by all Vajrayana or Tantric practitioners during daily meditation practice.

The bell is considered to be feminine and stands for wisdom about the true nature of reality. The dorje is male and represents the method or skillful means of living according to the teachings of compassionate action. During pujas and other ceremonies, the practitioner holds the bell in the left hand and the dorje in the right. The interaction of the bell and dorje symbolizes enlightenment, which is characterized as a perfect union of wisdom and method.

The sound produced by the bell is also considered to represent perfection. Further, the sound signifies the voice and spirit of the Buddha and the unified voice of the entire assembly of deities and enlightened beings. When Buddha's presence is felt in the room by the lama, the bell is rung as an offering.

MANTRAS AND THE HUMAN VOICE

The human voice is probably the best instrument for producing sounds to achieve specific purposes. Vibrations created by precise combinations of sounds have long been thought to affect both other living beings and inanimate objects.

The most powerful use of the voice in Buddhist belief is reciting a mantra. A *mantra* is a phrase or sentence, generally in Sanskrit or Tibetan, the sound of which embodies the power of a Buddha, deity, or other spirit entity. Lamas, healers, and Tantric prac-

Here the bell and dorje are shown forged together into an eternal union, with the dorje forming the handle for the bell. The dorje, known also as the vajra or "diamond thunderbolt" represents the indestructible and eternal. Its use symbolizes the destruction of the root of all disease, which is, of course, ignorance. The bell's hollow represents the "wisdom realizing emptiness." The bell's clapper represents the sound of emptiness. These two instruments are symbols of inner states of being which can be awakened by the practitioner and directed for many purposes, including healing.

titioners use mantras to cure disease, appease spirits, bring about good luck or other positive fortune, clear obstacles, and for many other reasons. Mantras can also be used for destructive purposes. Stories abound in Tibetan folklore of practitioners directing special mantras at living creatures to injure or even kill them.

Some Sanskrit mantras are so old that their original meanings have long been forgotten by most, perhaps all of the practitioners who use them. Other mantras are believed to be so powerful that they are held in secret by their possessors and revealed only to those who posess sufficient merit.

Professor Lama Chimpa helped me understand the mechanics of mantras. Uttering a mantra, he said, causes a special effect, something like a chemical reaction in the surrounding environment. The reaction is the result of a specific vibration caused by the utterance. Everyone knows that a certain note sung by a powerful singer can shatter a crystal glass, or that an army marching in unison across a bridge can destroy it. The effect of a mantra is created in a similar way.

The lama further explained that each mantra is composed of a specific sequence of sounds to produce a specific result. The process has been compared to mixing paints. Combining red and blue paint produces purple. Mixing the syllables *AH*, *OH*, and *MM* to produce *OM* also produces a special effect. Initiates into this art, known as Mantrayana, build up a repertoire of sound combinations, each designed to produce a unique effect. Lama Chimpa cautioned that there is no room for error when using mantras; mistakes using seed syllable combinations can have unfortunate consequences, he told me.

Moreover, mantras are said to derive their power from the inner attitude of the practitioner. Thus the intention of the person using them is the real source of mantra power. Considered in this way, mantras can be regarded as spiritual songs which spring from the heart rather than a dutiful repetition of a few syllables.

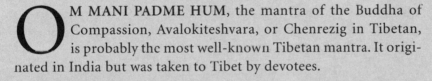

OM MANI PADME HUM, the mantra of the Buddha of Compassion, Avalokiteshvara, or Chenrezig in Tibetan, is probably the most well-known Tibetan mantra. It originated in India but was taken to Tibet by devotees.

Interpretations of the meaning of these four words are endless. A simplified and literal translation is "Hail, to the Jewel in the Lotus," but the symbolism connected with each word is profound.

OM represents the all-pervasive consciousness—the body, speech, and mind of the enlightened beings. This intelligence informs the universe. When OM is uttered, it resonates with the highest powers of universal order.

MANI, the jewel, is a symbol of the potential in human evolution for the highest attainment, cosmic consciousness. It also stands for the method of compassion—the highest ethic of sentient life.

PADME is the lotus. As a water plant, it is rooted in the mud, symbol of our ordinary or deluded state of consciousness, yet its flower reaches above the surface of the water toward the sunlight— a metaphor for the true nature of reality.

The lotus plant is also a metaphor for the subtle energy system of the human body. A refined energy is said to lie dormant at the base of the spine. When activated, it moves upward through the central channel, which parallels the spine, to the crown chakra at the top of the head. This energy enables the development of special psychic abilities. The energy itself is known as *kundalini* and is said by many to be the vehicle which enables our continuing evolution.

HUM represents integration—the union of the body, speech, and mind of the enlightened beings with our own body, speech, and mind, and the union of the method of compassion with the wisdom of the true nature of reality.

There are many stories about the magical uses of mantra in healing and to keep away illness, exhaustion, cold, hunger, and disease. One of these maintains that through their use, an experienced practitioner can disintegrate a physical object or even a living being. In the Devil-Dancing ceremonies of Ceylon, fire-cooling mantras are used to "tame" the fire for fire-walkers.[11]

Mantras are also used, sometimes accompanied by other practices, to enable practitioners known as *lung-gompas* to travel extremely quickly over difficult terrain, moving both day and night until a destination is reached. Another well-known effect linked to mantra practice enables lamas to create an inner body heat known as *tumo*, which enables their bodies to withstand subzero temperatures without suitable clothing.

One account indicates that, in the past, students had to demonstrate their mastery of this technique by sitting on a solid block of ice in the dead of winter until it melted.

Mantras are also among the most ancient healing techniques. As I noted in Chapter 2, one very important use of mantra for healers is in invoking the Medicine Buddha to bless medicines or produce other healing effects. Mantras are also dedicated to healing specific illnesses or to bring about specific results such as long life, clearing obstacles from one's life path, spiritually purifying food and offerings, and so on.

One very interesting story about how mantras are used in healing concerns the use of the *purbha*, a three-sided magic dagger often used for the "ritual slaying" of psychic foes. The Tamang Healer is well known for his use of the purbha in healing rituals. Sometimes he holds the ritual instrument on the crown of a patient's head while reciting a special mantra. The ritual is performed to expel the evil forces believed to have caused the illness. At other times, he holds the purbha over different chakras or energy centers on the body.

Tantric practitioners also are known to hold up the purbha in front of themselves, symbolically dividing any malevolent psychic force into two parts which are then deflected harmlessly away. In such cases, it is as if the mantras are used to empower the instrument itself.

A purbha, a three-sided magic dagger, is often used in healing rituals in conjunction with mantras. It's purpose is to expel evil forces or psychic obstacles.

Milarepa's Song

One of the great Tibetan masters of mantra was Jetsun (meaning "holy") Milarepa. A poet, saint, and yogi, Milarepa had the curious habit of replying to questions about the dharma in lyrical poetry or songs which he composed in the spirit of the moment. Many of these are recorded in the collection known as *The Hundred Thousand Songs of Milarepa*.

In the following song, Milarepa reminds us of our true nature, our destiny, and what is important in this life. In so doing, he supplies us with the Medicine of the Dharma.

We sentient beings moving in the world
Float down the stream
Of the Four sufferings [birth, age, sickness, death].
Compared to this, how much more formidable
Are the unceasing future lives in Samsara.
Why not, then, prepare a boat for the "crossing"?

The state of our future lives is far more fearful
And deserving of far more concern
Than are the dreadful demons, ghosts, and Yama [Lord of Death].
So why not prepare for yourself a guide?
Even the dread passions—craving, hatred and blindness—
Are not so fearful as the state of our
        (unknown) future,
So why not prepare for yourself an antidote?

Great is the Kingdom of the Three Realms
    of Samsara,
But greater is the endless road of birth-and-death,
So why not prepare for yourself provisions?
It will be better that you practice Dharma
If you have no assurance in yourselves. [12]

Mantra Machines

The power of mantras is harnessed by various techniques. As well as being recited, chanted, or sung, mantras are affixed to wheels, flags, the bottoms of shoes, and many other "machines," including nowadays, of course, computers. These machines allow mantras to be recited continuously, to assuage the suffering of beings in the lower realms of samsara and to produce other positive effects.

Lama Chimpa told an interesting story which demonstrates the relationship between a mantra's power and the mental attitude of the person using it. Some time ago, there were two monks of roughly equal knowledge and ability. One was an optimist, while the other was continually doubtful and negative. One day, the two friends were having a discussion. The optimist said, "Using this new mantra that our teacher has given

A mantra is engraved into a huge prayer wheel in Bodhnath. Each time the prayer wheel is turned clockwise, the mantra is released to do its munificent work in the universe. If the wheel is turned in a counterclockwise direction, however, a negative effect can result.

us, I will be able to put this knife right through the middle of that rock, and do it within a day." The other said, "No, it will take at least a week." With that, the two went their separate ways.

The very next morning, each began work on the task. Sure enough, on the first day, the optimist split the rock with the knife. After a week of struggle, his friend did the same. Conviction is the key to the successful use of mantras, concluded Lama Chimpa. Nothing is more powerful than the mind.

Mani Rilbu

Tibetan medical pills have traditionally been blessed by lamas. Such blessing are believed to increase their potency. These precious pills contain 25 ingredients, including old turquoise, coral, and pearls which are purified of their toxic content.

Barbara Gerke had a story to tell about mantras as well. Once every year, at a particular monastery in Dharamsala, a group of monks gathers to make Mani Rilbu. *Mani* refers to the "jewel" in the mantra of Chenrezig. The word *Rilbu* simply means "pill." Jewel pills are a Tibetan herbal medicine that has been consecrated using the OM MANI PADME HUM mantra. For several days, a group of lamas, together with lay practitioners, perform a recitation of this mantra over a huge quantity of pills, blessing them and endowing them with the qualities of the mantra. When they are finished, each of the practitioners is given a certain quantity. Small packets are also given to visitors to the monastery.

One day, early on in her studies in Dharamsala, Barbara met an old monk who had with him a certain number of these pills. As the two parted company, the monk handed her three of these special pills. On the advice of her friend, Barbara promptly swallowed them, not know-

ing a thing about either their purpose or the ceremony behind their creation. Nor did she know much about mantras. As she relates it, shortly afterward she found herself in a great state of happiness, dancing down the hill toward town, strangely enough reciting the Mani mantra.

Prayer Flags

Everywhere Tibetans live, you will find prayer flags. They are hung from roofs, displayed in yards, and festooned around monasteries and near prayer towers or *stupas*. They even flap in the wind at remote mountain passes far from any habitation. Sometimes you see them fluttering from vertical masts made of bamboo. Others are strung on long vertical lines stretched between two trees, roof posts, or other strategic places.

In Tibet, the custom dates to the eleventh century when the Indian saint, Atisha, first introduced it. Flags come in five colors, each representing a particular element. Blue is for water, red for fire, green for earth, yellow for wind and white for space.

Special divination practices enable lamas to determine whether these elements are deficient or in excess in people and sometimes in a particular geographical area. Then, the appropriate colors are selected to rectify the elemental imbalance.

Color therapy for the earth, however, is only one way in which flags are used. Each flag is also inscribed with sacred syllables or mantras. The idea is that when these flags are raised with pure intention, they become an instrument to bring benefit to the world. When touched by the wind,

If you can tear yourself away from the flapping of the prayer flags, and the beauty of the temples, on a clear day you might also see the high, snowy peaks of the Himalayas in the distance.

the fluttering of the flags releases the power of the mantras.

In terms of personal healing, a Tibetan astrological reading provides a detailed calculation of the elements as they relate to us, for each day, month, and year of our lives. The resulting chart indicates which of these elements are weak and need to be strengthened to avoid serious illness. Raising the appropriately colored prayer flags on the correct days is believed to strengthen this element, reducing the chances of related diseases. Of course, this ritual must be conducted with full devotion, concentration, and in accordance with tradition. Raising prayer flags on the wrong day, for example, is said to have disastrous consequences.

Perhaps the most memorable prayer flag scene I came upon was at the top of Darjeeling Hill. Here there are three temples, Hindu, Christian, and Buddhist. Before the arrival of the British, this region was part of Sikkim and largely Buddhist. Naturally, since it was built first, the Buddhist temple has the most favorable location, on the very top of the hill.

The British built a Christian church nearby, and after they left, Hindus built a shrine here, too. Unfortunately, these groups have not always lived together in harmony, and over the years there has been some conflict. Still, devotees of all three faiths can be found on Darjeeling Observatory Hill at any time.

Aside from its historic interest, the visitor who makes the pilgrimage to the top of the hill is in for another treat. The trees and architectural objects near the Buddhist shrine are covered with a multitude of prayer flags. In itself, this is not an unusual sight. But the ropes from which the flags are suspended are used by monkeys who climb them as they please. Each day, a troupe of monkeys moves up the mountainside to the hilltop because they know tourists will feed them. Emboldened by years of exposure to the public, these creatures let observers approach to within a few feet.

OTHER RITUAL OBJECTS AND TECHNIQUES

Mudras

In any thangka or other representation of a Buddhist deity or historical teacher, you will see the hands of the principle figure making a symbolic gesture called a *mudra*. These gestures actually comprise a symbolic language which communicates key messages. Mudras are used by lamas and other Tantric practitioners during initiations, daily meditation practice, offering ceremonies or pujas, and other ritual occasions.

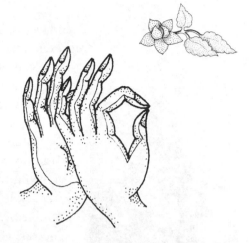

The expertise required to use mudras smoothly and gracefully requires practice. This expertise is necessary because mudras attempt to portray perfection.

Mudras are performed at the same time as a mantra is recited. A translation of the second line of the Medicine Buddha mantra which would accompany this mudra is roughly, "OM! Medicine Buddha, King of Medicine, accept this water for your feet. My salutations to you."

Visualization Practices

Tibetan visualization practices are complex and elaborate mental exercises. Practitioners build layer upon layer of specific scenes before their mind's eye.

The touching thumb and index fingers of the right hand represent the union of wisdom and method, the two causes that bring about Buddhahood. At their source, these two causes have the desire to attain a state of liberation for the sake of all sentient beings. For this state to manifest, we must first develop the determination to be free from the sufferings of samsara.

The three raised fingers represent the Three Baskets of the Buddha's teachings. Simply hearing the dharma, it is said, can lead sentient beings to the path, which has three stages or goals according to the capacity of the practitioner: (1) the desire for a better future life; (2) the desire to free oneself permanently from samsaric suffering; and (3) the intention to seek Buddhahood so as to help free all beings from samsaric suffering. The left hand represents the beings of the three capacities themselves, who follow the path of method and wisdom.

Each layer is filled with beings, forms, colors, and sacred words which represent dharma concepts. For instance, a practitioner might visualize the complex mandala or sacred abode of a Buddha, the lineage tree of historical masters of a particular practice, or the syllables of a mantra complete with brilliant color and exquisite sound.

Studying thangka paintings gives you some idea of the scope and variety of Buddhist imagination in this area. In a typical Medicine Buddha thangka, for instance, the Medicine Buddha is blue in color. He holds a begging bowl in his left hand and a sprig of the Noble Myrobalan plant in his right. The bowl is filled with healing nectar which represents the medicine of the dharma. Everything about the Buddha's form and its surroundings, throne, other deities, environment, and so on, is richly detailed and replete with symbolism. Practitioners try to hold all of these associations in mind simultaneously with the vivid mental picture.

Visualization exercises have many purposes. Perhaps foremost is that they offer a systematic way of transmitting the esoteric meaning of dharma teachings. Ultimately, the beings and environments envisioned represent advanced states of consciousness and correspondingly superior states of physical and mental well-being. Through practice, the student experiences these noble characteristics and attempts to emulate them "on the cushion" as well as in life between meditation sessions.

Lama Tenzin Yignyen of Namgyal Monastery demonstrates the mudra representing a water offering for the feet. The palm of his left hand is turned down, and his right hand, with the index finger pointed outward, represents a conch shell holding water. This mudra can be traced to the hot climate pervasive throughout much of India—hence the idea of water to cool the feet of an honored guest.

The idea of mental images assuming material form or influencing the material world is commonly accepted in Tibetan medicine. As we have seen, it is our thoughts, which give rise to words and deeds, that are the root cause of our afflictions. But our thoughts can also redeem us. Ultimately, the purpose of visualization practices is to bring about our own liberation from

suffering and the liberation of others.

Modern visualization practices, not directly related to Buddhism, are based on the recognition of the utility of mental imagery. These methods are very practical and attempt to bring about the healing and prevention of many different diseases. Though these techniques are new to modern medicine, they are ancient elsewhere in the world. Often in conjunction with the use of mantras and meditation, visualization practices are now commonly cultivated by people diagnosed with a wide range of medical problems.

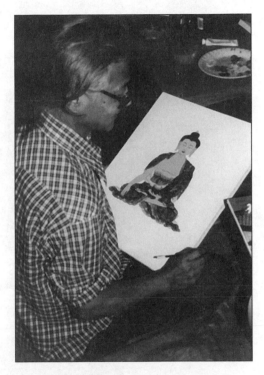

Some theories maintain that by using these techniques, practitioners are able to gain control over their own immune systems, thereby participating in the healing process at a conscious level. Practitioners of these methods see themselves not merely as helpless victims of unknowable, unassailable forces but as capable agents willing and able to make a difference in their own recovery.

Tibetan artist Karma Phuntsok working with a student's painting. He explained the relationship of his paintings to healing in the following way:

"My paintings are not pills, but they work in similar ways. My work is like medicine, a medicine for the mind. My paintings challenge their owners to think. What is this Being? What is its meaning? Where does it originate? Why is it important?

"This work also brings about peace. My paintings are popular with psychologists and social workers. These people put them in their offices and waiting rooms because they occupy the attention [of clients] and even soothe them."

The Gomchen's Observation

The "reality" of images we have visualized and their power to hurt or heal us is the subject of this dialogue between the intrepid lady adventurer, Alexandra David-Neel, and a Tibetan gomchen (meditation master) of her acquaintance. Terrifying mental images were often used to develop complete fearlessness in young lamas; however, tradition holds that some horrific images actually scared unlucky novices to death.

"It is only prudent", he cautioned, "to beware of opening [subtle] channels without due consideration. Few, indeed, suspect what the great storehouse of the world which they tap unconsciously, contains. . . . One must know how to protect oneself from the tigers to which one has given birth as well as against those that have been begotten by others."

The gomchen also mentioned that we humans are not the only beings capable of creating entities with the mind and that these beings roam the earth fulfilling the purposes their creators set. We could easily meet such creatures in our daily lives, he warned. By the fruits of our own actions, he concluded, we create conditions through which we may encounter them.[13]

CHAPTER NINE

Divination and Shamanic Healing

There is something compelling about a bag of bones. More gripping still is using them to see the future. The practice of divination has always been a mysterious art, one whose secrets have been carefully guarded. Although I intuitively recognized its potential value, I had never understood how divination might actually work.

I knew that Tibetans, like Native Americans and other peoples around the world, derive meaning from natural occurrences—a crow flying west, a rainbow in a clear sky—as well as from various formal methods of divination such as the pattern made by a bag of animal bones cast on the ground. But though I wanted to believe that such things had significance, I could not do so without a rationale.

During my interview with the Tibetan astrologer, Mrs. Choezom from Men Tsee Khang, I discovered that certain types of divination were completely integrated into astrological practice. These techniques include the eight trigrams so prominent in the famous Chinese text, the *I Ching*. Other ancient systems of divination used by the Tibetan astrologer include the five elements, the nine magic square numbers, and the twelve animal signs. Together with the trigrams, these methods are used to make predictions about many aspects of life.

I also found out that historically, divination practices were closely aligned with the traditional medical practice, so much so, that like

shamans and lamas, professional astrologers were regularly sought out to perform divinations under certain conditions. Long-term illnesses, for example, that did not respond to conventional treatment were often assumed to have karmic or spirit world origins. These types of medical problems were diagnosed and prescribed for using divination techniques.

Using divination methods, the lama, shaman, or astrologer would determine whether the disease could be cured and what type of medicines should be used. A friend told me the following story:

"I remember that when I fell sick in Dharamsala in 1990, a Lama did a Mo. He told me that the disease was caused by a Naga [serpent spirit of the underworld] who was disturbed by the construction of the newly built house I was living in at the time. The house had been constructed near the spring where it lived.

"The Mo also gave information on what kind of pujas needed to be done to pacify the spirit and to improve my health. Further, the divination revealed that Tibetan medicine would not help in this case and that I had to take allopathic medicines. I did do the pujas but did not want to take allopathic medicines.

"Unfortunately, it was true that Tibetan medicines would not help, despite my having consulted the best Tibetan doctors available. I finally met a Great Lama who 'blew' mantras onto my face and gave me mantra water with saffron to drink and to sprinkle throughout the house. He also gave me clay blessed with mantras to put on my open wounds. I was cured within a week.

"I also was told to invite monks from the monastery to my house to perform a Naga Puja. This I did. Not a single scar remained on my skin from these rather severely infected wounds."

Known in Tibetan as *Mo*, divination is a means for us to know things

that are currently hidden from our understanding. The key to the system is remembering that since we exist in the samsaric realm, our perceptions are incomplete and imperfect. Our inability to perceive the relationships between particular phenomena, such as signs pointing to the manifestation of a disease, does not mean that such a relationship does not exist. It only means that due to ignorance, *ma-rig-pa*, we cannot recognize it.

Several years ago, I requested an interview with two Tibetan lamas, Lama Inge Zangmo and Lama Yontan Gonpo, to help explain the use of divination. The ensuing discussion gave me a clearer sense of how Tibetan divination actually works. Tibetans, they explained, have traditionally used any number of tools to divine. These include tortoise shells, butter lamps, astrological charts, and crow augury. Each of these methods has its own special system of interpretation which yields a specific range of ideas for consideration. In crow augury, decisions are made on the basis of the behavior or cries of that bird when it is first sighted by the diviner.

As interpreted by trained individuals, these devices help to clarify relationships which cannot normally be perceived. Tibetan astrologers typically classify these relationships into such categories as spiritual matters, family, health, finance, and evil spirits. Divinations are performed not only to help us prepare for unavoidable situations but also to give us a general sense of our coming fortune.

Divination is also used to suggest the proper method of disposal of a corpse. One divination system keyed to the five elements is used to determine which of five burial types is appropriate. Depending on which element appears in the divination, the message is that the corpse should be cremated (fire), buried (earth), placed in water (water), interred beneath the house (iron), or exposed for "sky burial" by vultures (wood).

Ultimately, however, it is not the method or the corresponding system of interpretation that is important. As the lamas were to explain,

what is of real importance to a successful divination is the state of mind and the level of spiritual attainment of the diviner.

An Interview with Lama Inge and Lama Yontan

Lama Inge: Divination is a science, an occult science. A catalog arrived the other day. This catalog is filled with spiritual and occult books— pages and pages—astrology, tarot, palmistry, numerology. They all work. Basically, the principle of divination—the highest point of understanding—is that whatever appears, any phenomenon, is a display of wisdom. Any phenomenon has meaning, and it is for you to find out that meaning. That is divination.

Lama Yontan: If we were at one with that display, with that wisdom, with the essential nature of everything that exists, there would be no need for divination, we would just know. So, whatever the method of divination, it is simply a means to take us momentarily out of our habitual [thinking] pattern and plug us into that awareness. It is a way of getting around egocentric grasping or clinging to the truth.

Inge: There are countless methods. It could be tea leaves or clouds or the way a butterfly flies or birds. The Romans used birds; crow augury—the word *augury* comes from birds. So whatever it is, it elicits meaning in our minds.

Yontan: In the Tibetan language [this meaning] would be called *rig-pa*, "great knowing." [Divination is] a way of connecting with rig-pa, of overcoming our habitual tendencies of remaining in ordinary mind, so that we can connect with Great Mind.

One of the most subtle means of divination that we have—and we all have it, and we all use it and don't realize it—is intuition. Things come into our mind, and we either pay attention or we don't. If we pay attention, we say, "Oh, that's intuitive." And if we don't, well, that's ordinary mind.

In the process of mind training, intuition is the link between intellect and awareness. It is actually a form of divination.

Most lamas will use their *mala* [prayer beads] or they have developed different methods. Actually there was one Mo that Rinpoche [Chagdud Tulku Rinpoche] put together in a Gompa in Cottage Grove [Oregon] at one time. It's still there. You ask a question and then this deep bowl is full of sticks and you whirl them around. Whirl them and whirl them and whirl them and whirl them. One flies out. You grab that one, get its number, go to the sheet describing the number, and it gives you an answer. That's one traditional Tibetan method.

Inge: What appears to be a random process is not really random at all. That is where you are in the moment. The one stick that

flies out is the display of wisdom. That's how everything works, the coins for the *I Ching*, the dice for the Mo. Understanding in this way requires a certain confidence, a "knowing" and a total openness.

SHAMANIC HEALING

Divination practices are often—perhaps always—used in shamanic healing rituals. The shaman uses divination to discover the source of the disease and then how best to combat it. Shamanic healing methods have evolved over centuries, perhaps millennia, in the Himalayan region of Tibet. These practices are quite different from the monastic practices of the lamas, although they may hold some origins in common.

Late one afternoon, the evening before my departure from Nepal, I found myself in the second-story office of Dr. Rita Prasad Gartoulla, a social anthropologist currently working in Bodhnath. I had tried to meet him since my arrival, but circumstances had not, until now, been favorable.

I first heard of Dr. Gartoulla and his work in medical anthropology the year before. He was at that time associated with an American organization, "Ventures in Peace," dedicated to improving health, education, and living standards among the Nepali people.

During our conversation about traditional healing, the subject of shamanism came up. Dr. Gartoulla told me that he had studied this group of healers extensively. There were, he said, at least thirteen distinct types of shamans in the Himalayan region. The practices of the various groups differ widely. Some shamans sacrifice animals during their rituals; others use only flowers or grains.

The spirits invoked by the shamans of this region were not always beneficent. In the eighth century, Padmasambhava, the Tantric master from India, was invited to Tibet to establish Buddhism in the region. A previous attempt to import the dharma to the region had been a failure. Though King Trisong Detsen had invited the scholar Santarakshita, also from the south, to bring the dharma to Tibet, as legend has it, his mission failed because of the powerful demonic forces native to the region.

Padmasambhava, who followed Santarakshita, succeeded. He not only subdued the demons, but he enlisted them as helpers and protectors of the dharma. These same subdued spirits could be summoned by shamans to assist them in curing diseases.

After hearing Dr. Gartoulla's stories, I resolved to make a final attempt to meet a certain shamanic healer I had heard about some time before. I desperately wanted to see this practice in action for myself. I succeeded in my goal in a most spectacular and unusual way. Not two hours before my flight home left Katmandu, I watched a Tibetan shamaness at work. In fact, she worked on me. Here's what happened.

THE LHAMO DOLKER

Early in my trip, I had visited Ian Baker, an author living in Katmandu. He had recently written a book on Tibetan medicine, and I hoped he could offer some leads. We met at his house, down a quiet alley, two hundred yards beyond the temple of the dancing goblins at the Naxal crossroads.

During our conversation, Ian mentioned something he had witnessed some years before. A shamaness, he said, the Lhamo Dolker, lived not far from where I was staying in Bodhnath. She was very famous, and people from all over Europe and India as well as Nepal came to her for healing.

He had watched the Lhamo as she had bitten a patient on the stomach. Before his eyes, she had sucked out some evil-looking substance. She treated a number of patients in exactly that way during a morning session. By the time she finished, she had filled a large bowl with a vile-looking poison. From his unobstructed point of view in the room, Ian had watched the process from beginning to end. If you want to see a real shaman in action, he said, here's how to find her.

Several days later, in the broad light of day, I tried to follow Ian's directions to the Lhamo's apartment: Walk along main street in Bodhnath towards the Stupa but on the opposite side of the road. When you come to a water pump, look around for an alley. Walk the alley to the end, turn left. There you will see steps leading into a building. The Lhamo is on the third floor.

The Lhamo's alley in the teeming streets of Bodhnath.

After a couple of tries, I found the water pump, the alley, and the apartment. The healer, however, was on an extended trip to India. The sign on her door, tactfully placed behind a cotton curtain, read, "The Lhamo is in India for three months. She will return in May."

I was crestfallen, since it was still April. Ian's account had been captivating, horrifying as it was, and I determined that whatever else, I would meet her before leaving Nepal. Periodically, I checked the apartment for signs of her return until leaving for India a month later. But luck, it seemed, had abandoned me. After taking some photos of her alley and her sign, I reluctantly moved on to India.

When I returned to Nepal, my trip nearing its conclusion, my luck changed. The morning before my flight was to leave, I tried again. After climbing the three floors, I was once again greeted by the padlock on her door and the familiar sign, now a little faded, announcing her absence.

I took out my camera to photograph the sign, certain it would be my only momento of shamanic healing. Just as I was about to press the shutter, a man in his thirties brushed past me, took out a key, and started to open the door. "Are you looking for the Lhamo?" he asked.

"Yes," I replied hopefully, "I am."

"Come back tomorrow at nine in the morning, and she will be here," the fellow said, as he disappeared behind the curtain into the house.

By ten minutes to nine the next morning, the Lhamo's apartment was already full. Eleven people were crowded into a small room. Four were Westerners. Later, I found out that often twice as many people are jammed into that same space. The same fellow I had met the day before brought us tea. Gradually, the group relaxed, and a silence fell upon us.

Just as the last cup of tea was finished, the Lhamo made her appearance. She was dressed in traditional Tibetan garments, her full-length dress sweeping the floor as she moved past us. After a few words in confidence to her helper, she moved to a corner where she stood before a large thangka, one of many hanging on the walls. This painting portrayed Manjushri, his flaming sword of wisdom ready to cut through ignorance.

Here the Lhamo conducted her preliminary rituals and made offerings. Still standing, she began to utter strange unearthly cries and shrieks, which occasionally softened into hauntingly beautiful melodies. These sounds filled the little room and, as the hair gradually rose higher on the back of my neck, she seemed to slip into a trance, looking to my

eyes much larger, more massive and powerful than she had a few moments before. I felt certain that she had successfully invoked her spirits.

Soon, the Lhamo sat before us in the lotus position. Her assistant explained what would occur: one by one, we would sit before the Lhamo. While still in a trace, she would then diagnose and treat us. Somehow she had discovered I had to leave within the hour, because before I realized it, I was bumped, reluctant and protesting, to the head of the line. I had intended simply to watch and vainly tried to explain this to the assistant, as the Lhamo Dolker did not speak English.

However, she seemed to want to examine me. In fact, she insisted. Since everyone else in the room was impatiently waiting a turn, I soon submitted. Taking my pulse in Tibetan style, she correctly diagnosed an old injury to my spine. I began to pay close attention.

A Tibetan shamaness in full ritual regalia uses sound to enter a trance state.

The injury was, she continued, more acute in the cold season than in the hot, and that it had originated many years earlier in some type of labor-related accident. She then asked me to turn around and, pulling my shirt out of the way, began to study the area. Though I could not see her working, I got the impression of a scientist at work.

Soon she began to probe along each of the lower vertebrae with something very hard and sharp—a long fingernail perhaps. The probing was actually very painful, and it continued for some time. So painful and persistent was it that, to my embarrassment, I began groaning.

Finally, her assistant held in front of me a small bowl of discolored fluid. This substance, he claimed, had been removed by the Lhamo from between the vertebrae along lower reaches of my spine. As I was contemplating the contents of the bowl, I heard a scream from the back of the room, "Oh, God, she's going to bite him." As I looked up to see where this call had come from, I was bitten on my backside, just to one side of my spine. The bite was centered directly over a calcified lump, barely visible, but the only observable evidence of my injury.

Exactly how long the bite lasted is difficult to say. All I really remember about it is the pain and the fact that her grip seemed to strengthen over time. I have already mentioned the pain from her initial probing, but that seemed nothing as compared to the experience of being bitten. When her assistant finally showed me the vile and discolored results, I carefully searched the bowl for small pieces of vertebrae which I was certain would be floating somewhere in the pool. Finding none, I tried my best to ignore the acute discomfort and listened to her synopsis.

The Lhamo Dolker's Diagnosis

• My back problem had been caused by an industrial accident many years earlier.

• The problem became more acute in winter.

• The substance she had removed from along the spinal column was stagnant blood which had been trapped there.

• I should not drink cold liquids.

- I must not do heavy physical work in the future.

- My lower back should be massaged regularly with various oils.

- I was to eat small amounts of wheat grain which she had blessed.

After studying me for some time, the last thing she said through her translator, was this: "You think too much. This is not good. Stop thinking! Slowly, slowly," she continued using hand gestures to emphasize her idea, "you will get better."

At this, everyone in the room burst out laughing, myself included. Although her words themselves didn't convey the specific meaning, the message itself was crystal clear. "Pay more attention to your feelings and the *lung* energy that makes you so restless will gradually subside and stop afflicting your mind."

I left the room to the sounds of the next patient's screams, saluting the Lhamo as I did, and rushed to the guesthouse where the taxi to the airport was waiting. I had plenty of time over the next few days to think about my visit to the Lhamo, since to make the return journey, I had to take four different jets.

Over the next few days, try as I might to reflect on my Asian experience, I found my thoughts returning again and again to the shamaness and my experiences in her apartment. Perhaps it was the pain from the bite that kept me focused on her words, for I found that the wound was especially sensitive to rubbing against what otherwise would have been comfortable airplane seats.

Weeks passed, and the wound finally healed. Nothing much of the

experience was left except a vivid memory and a ring of bite marks on my backside. Even now, many months later, I still wonder, from time to time, whether the Lhamo Dolker's treatment actually worked. I can only say that while the calcified lump has not mysteriously disappeared, it has not bothered me either.

CHAPTER TEN

Prayer to the Noble Tara

My encounter with the Lhamo Dolker had convinced me that Tibetans knew all about ferocity and passion in their healing rituals. I can still picture the shamaness, larger than life, a tremendous, looming figure moving rhythmically with the flow of mighty, invisible forces. The whole experience seemed somehow to link me to the not-so-distant past, a time when every village or clan had a shaman.

But after all was said and done, it was the mystical pole of the Tibetan healing arts that won me over. This spiritual side was more sacred than magical, more gentle than violent, more refined than crude. It was here, I believed, that the authentic spirit of Tibetan Buddhist healing could be found. And it was this spirit that informed the practice of shamans, lamas, and physicians alike.

The wisdom of Tibetan Buddhist practice, the rituals, prayers, initiations, and their supportive arts and techniques, have not changed in millennia. The philosophical ideas which underlie this complex system of practice are as relevant today as they were in days long past. This is curious, since everything else around us seems to be changing with tremendous rapidity. This paradox suggests that at an ontological level, at the core of human experience, there is a something constant. From this eternal center, the great teachers looked deeply into the condition of humanity and prescribed healing medicine to remedy its ills.

This medicine is especially important today, in that period of human history known as the "end times." Buddhists believe that we today live in a "degenerated age" in which our relentless pursuit of material pleasures brings about massive problems, including many new diseases. The great medical and spiritual teachers of the past were well aware that the woes of our current era would descend on us. In their compassion, they offered both medical treatments and spiritual practices like that of Medicine Buddha to help us cope with the ills of body and spirit that would arise.

One of the most useful insights from these teachings is the idea that disease, illness, disharmony, and misfortunes of all types are useful tools for investigating personal and societal circumstances. Essentially, unpleasant life situations can be regarded as clues which we can use to bring about a deeper understanding of ourselves and of our relationship with the world. By using misfortune as a gauge to our inner state of being, we motivate ourselves to improve our lives and the lives of those around us.

Seen in this way, negative situations can be regarded as blessings. The primacy of this task—to investigate one's personal condition and to bring about changes where necessary—is clearly stated throughout the dharma, as in the following paraphrase: "By one's self, the evil is done; by one's self, one suffers; by one's self, evil is left undone; by one's self one is purified. The pure and the impure stand and fall by themselves; no one can purify another."[14]

Extending this, we see that problems, including health challenges, compel us to face circumstances which we would otherwise ignore. These confrontations, in turn, compel us to look at life in new ways. A family friend once told me that as far as he was concerned, the principle effect of his cancer, which proved to be fatal, was to open him to new realms of consciousness.

In Tibetan lore, these higher states of consciousness are personified

by a pantheon of gods and goddesses. One figure in particular stands apart—Tara, known in various forms the world over. This radiant goddess embodies all that is helpful, compassionate, fearless, and healing. Representing the feminine aspect of the Buddha-Nature, Tara is understood to be the Buddha-Mother. Known as "She Who Saves," Tara is also the protectoress of the sick. She is the most central female deity in the Tibetan system, and all female healing goddesses are thought to emanate from her.

According to legend, Tara had been a human woman who vowed to work towards the liberation of all sentient beings. She further vowed to achieve enlightenment in female form and to remain in this form to be a helpful and healing mother figure for all beings in need. In her many aspects—white, green, red, wrathful, peaceful, twenty-one in all—Tara has become the most beloved of all Tibetan female deities.

Benoytosh Bhattacharyya, an Indian writer and philosopher, recounts a mystical encounter with Green Tara: "Every night I started repeating the Mantra [OM TARE TUTTARE TURE SOHA] with full concentration and with the utmost devotion in order to see if I could get any new experience. . . .After a full fortnight one day suddenly before my closed eyes flashed forth a strong white light, rather remarkable, and within that light I could see very clearly the figure of a goddess with green emerald colour so exquisitely beautiful in all limbs that it cannot be described in words. The deity sat in Lalitasana [a yogic posture reserved for enlightened beings, deities, and princes] on a double lotus and held in her left hand some leaves and in the right showed the Varada [gift bestowing] mudra with a gem of extreme brilliance. The deity stood before my eyes for a few seconds and disappeared into the white light."[15]

Tara has another extraordinary characteristic. Unlike other Tantric deities, she is directly accessible to all those who request her help, not simply to those who have been initiated into her practice tradition. Because I have been assured that Tara's healing blessings can help anyone

who calls on her sincerely, I would like to conclude with a short White Tara healing practice composed by Kyabje Gelek Rinpoche, the spiritual director of The Jewel Heart Center for Tibetan Culture and Buddhist Studies, based in Ann Arbor, Michigan.

The instructions for a simple visualization to accompany this practice are as follows: Visualize that Tara is sitting in front of you, just as she is described in the practice. As you repeat Tara's mantra, visualize that hook-like light rays go out from the syllables of the mantra at Tara's heart, reaching in ten directions to every part of every universe. The light rays return to Tara, bringing with them the purity, vigor, and capability of each of the five elements in their natural state. Imagine these rays streaming from Tara's heart to you, bathing you in brilliantly colored light and liquid.

Each of the element rays has its own color and healing energy:

● **Golden yellow** rejuvenates your Earth element and works with bodily strength, organs, flesh, and bones.

● **Milky white** rejuvenates your Water element and works with blood, body fluids, and emotions.

● **Orange-red** rejuvenates your Fire element and works with vital energy, heat, and digestion.

● **Emerald green** rejuvenates your Air element and works with the respiratory system, the wind humor, and mental agitation.

● **Sapphire blue** rejuvenates your Space element and creates mental spaciousness and room to accommodate all things.

You can also use this practice to heal, protect, and help others who are ill. Imagine these people sitting around you. The light and liquid streaming from Tara's heart reaches these figures, bathing them as well as you and granting them Tara's compassionate aid.

Prayer to the Noble Tara
by Kyabje Gelek Rinpoche

I and all sentient beings take refuge in the Buddha, Dharma, Sangha, Tara and her Mandala. (Repeat 3 times)

For the benefit of all sentient beings, in order to reach a state of perfection, I shall practice this prayer to the Noble Tara. (Repeat 3 times)

In the space before me appears a white lotus. Upon it, a moon disk; and upon that, the love and compassion of all the Enlightened Beings appears as the Noble Wish-Fulfilling Tara. She sits on a lotus

and moon cushion, a luminous moon halo at her back. Youthful and radiant, her right hand gestures an invitation to liberation. Her left hand, holding an utpala flower, indicates the protection of the Three Jewels, giving courage and assurance to those dominated by fear.

At her crown a white OM, at her throat a red AH, at her heart a white TAM marked by a blue HUM. Light radiates from the heart-syllable, inviting the wisdom beings and empowering deities. The wisdom beings unite inseparably with Tara. The empowering deities confer initiation. A Buddha of Infinite Life adorns her crown.

I bow down in body, speech, and mind.
I present offerings both actually arranged and mentally created.
I purify all deluded actions.
I rejoice in all pure activities.
I request you to remain until total enlightenment.
I request wise and compassionate guidance.
I dedicate my merit for the benefit of all beings.

Brilliant light radiates from within the syllable TAM within Tara's heart, collecting back the essence of inexhaustible vitality and powerful blessings of body, speech, and mind.

Energy streams forth from Tara's heart and body. I and all beings absorb this energy of light and are cleansed and revitalized, obtaining the realization of deathlessness.

OM TARE TUTTARE TURE SOHA
(Repeat as many times as possible with the visualization)

OM, I and all prostrate to the liberator, the fully realized transcendent subduer.
I prostrate to the glorious mother who liberates with TARE.
The mother who eliminates all fears with TUTTARE.
The mother who grants all success with TURE.
To SOHA and the other syllables I offer the greatest homage.

TARE MA liberates from samsara.
TUTTARE liberates from the eight fears.
TURE liberates from all illnesses.
To you, the great liberating mother, I prostrate.

If foreseeing signs of premature death, may I clearly perceive the Noble Tara and achieve the realization of deathlessness.

By this virtue may I quickly attain the essence of Tara and secure every being without exception in that state.[16]

Notes

1. W. Y. Evans-Wentz, *The Tibetan Book of the Dead* (New York: Oxford University Press, 1960), 91.

2. Tsewang Y. Pemba, *Young Days in Tibet* (London: Jonathan Cape, 1957), 25.

3. Lobsang Dolma Khangkar, *Lectures on Tibetan Medicine* (The Library of Tibetan Works and Archives, 1991), 58-82.

4. Lobsang Wangyal, "The Practice and Principle of Diagnosis in Tibetan Medicine," *Journal of the Tibetan Medical & Astrological Institute* 1, no. 1 (1995): 32.

5. From the Venerable Tenzin Gephel's discourse on "The Six Perfections," Namgyal Monastery, Ithaca, N.Y., Dec. 4-12, 1998.

6. Richard McKeon, ed., *The Basic Works of Aristotle* (New York: Random House, 1941), 403.

7. *Atharva-Veda*, trans. William Dwight Whitney (Delhi: Motilal Banarsidas, 1971), 2:498-501.

8. Ibid., 550.

9. *The Gyushi*. Translated by Barbara Gerke.

10. David Snellgrove, *The Nine Ways of Bon* (London: Oxford University Press, 1967), 37-39.

11. W. Y. Evans-Wentz, *Tibetan Yoga and Secret Doctrines* (London: Oxford University Press, 1973), 161.

12. *The Hundred Thousand Songs of Milarepa*, trans. Garma C. C. Chang (New York: University Books, 1962), 114-115.

13. Alexandra David-Neel, *Magic and Mystery in Tibet* (New York: Crown Publishers, 1937), 148.

14. *The Teachings of the Compassionate Buddha: Early Discourses, the Dhammapada, and Later Writings,* ed. E. A. Burtt (New York: The New American Library, 1955), 60.

15. Benoytosh Bhattacharyya, *An Introduction to Buddhist Esotericism* (Varanasi, India: The Chowkhamba Sanskrit Series Office, 1964), 7-8.

16. Unpublished practice composed by Ngawang Kyabje Gelek Rinpoche, Ann Arbor, Mich. Used by permission.

Bibliography

BIOGRAPHICAL

Barborka, Geoffrey A., *H.P. Blavatsky: Tibet and Tulku*. Madras, India:
The Theosophical Publishing House, 1966.

Blofeld, John, The Wheel of Life: *The Autobiography of a Western
Buddhist*. Boston: Shambhala Publications, 1988.

Kalsang, Lama Thubten (trans.) et. al., *Atisha: A Biography of the
Renowned Buddhist Sage*. New Delhi: Mahayana Publications, 1983.

Kohn, Sherab Chodzin, *The Awakened One: A Life of the Buddha*.
London: Phoenix, 1994.

BOTANICAL

Biswas, K., *Common Medicinal Plants of Darjeeling and the Sikkim
Himalayas*. Alipor, West Bengal: West Bengal Government Press,
1956.

Department of Medicinal Plants, *Medicinal Plants of Nepal: Bulletin of
the Department of Medicinal Plants,* 4th ed. Kathmandu, Nepal:
His Majesty's Government of Nepal, Ministry of Forests and Soil
Conservation, 1993.

Polunin, Oleg, and Adam Stainton, *Concise Flowers of the Himalaya*.
Delhi, India: Oxford University Press, 1997.

Tsarong, Tsewang J., *Tibetan Medicinal Plants*. Kalimpong, India:
Tibetan Medical Publications, 1994.

MEDICAL AND ASTROLOGICAL

Astrology Department, Tibetan Medical and Astrology Institute, *Tibetan Astronomy and Astrology: A Brief Introduction.* Dharamsala, India: Astrology Department, T.M.A.I., 1995.

Baker, Ian, *The Tibetan Art of Healing.* Illustrated by Romio Shrestha. San Francisco: Chronicle Books, 1997.

Donden, Yeshi, *Health Through Balance. An Introduction to Tibetan Medicine.* Ithaca: Snow Lion Publications, 1986.

Dummer, Tom, *Tibetan Medicine And Other Holistic Health-Care Systems.* London: Routledge, 1988.

Gerke, Barbara (ed.), *AyurVijnana: A Periodical on Indo-Tibetan and Allied Medical Cultures.* Kalimpong, West Bengal: International Trust for Traditional Medicine (ITTM), Volume 3, #2, August 1997.

Khangkar, Lobsang Dolma, *Lectures on Tibetan Medicine.* Library of Tibetan Works and Archives, 1986.

sMan-rTsis, *Journal of the Tibetan Medical & Astro. Institute.* 1, no. 1 (1995).

Parfionovitch, Yuri (ed.), et. al., *Tibetan Medical Paintings: Illustrations to the Blue Beryl Treatise of Sangye Gyamtso,* Vols. 1, 2. New York: H.N. Abrams, 1992.

Phrin-las, Byams-pa (trans.), et. al., *Tibetan Medical Thangka of the Four Medical Tantras.* People's Publishing House of Tibet, 1987.

Tiwari, Maya, *Ayurveda: A Life of Balance.* Rochester, Vt.: Healing Arts Press, 1995.

Zopa, Thubten Rinpoche, *The Healing Buddha: A Practice for the Prevention and Healing of Disease.* Boston: Wisdom Publications, 1994.

TECHNICAL

Chagdud Tulku Rinpoche, *Red Tara: An Open Door to Bliss and Ultimate Awareness.* Junction City, Cal.: Padma Publishing, 1991.

Dagyab Rinpoche, *Buddhist Symbols in Tibetan Culture.* Boston: Wisdom Publications, 1995.

Gelek Rinpoche, *Prayer to the Noble Tara.* Monograph, n.d.

Gyatrul Rinpoche, *Ancient Wisdom: Nyingma Teachings on Dream Yoga: Meditation and Transformation.* Ithaca: Snow Lion Publications, 1993.

Jackson, David, and Janice Jackson, *Tibetan Thangka Painting: Methods and Materials.* Ithaca: Snow Lion Publications, 1988.

Jansen, Eva Rudy, *Singing Bowls: A Practical Handbook of Instruction and Use.* Diever, Holland: Binkey Kok Publications, 1994.

Nebesky-Wejkowitz, Rene de, *Oracles and Demons in Tibet: The Cult and Iconography of Tibetan Protective Deities.* London: Oxford University Press, 1956.

Norbu, Namkhai, *Dream Yoga and the Practice of Natural Light.* Ithaca: Snow Lion Publications, 1992.

Travel

Chan, Victor. *Tibet Handbook*. Chico, California: Moon Publications, 1994.

Coxall, Michelle, and Paul Greenway, *Indian Himalaya: A Lonely Planet Travel Survival Kit*. Hawthorne, Australia: Lonely Planet Publications, 1996.

David-Neel, Alexandra. *Magic and Mystery in Tibet*. New York: Crown Publishers, 1937.

Finlay, Hugh, Richard Everist, and Tony Wheeler, *Nepal: A Lonely Planet Travel Survival Kit*. Hawthorne, Vic., Australia: Lonely Planet Publications, 1996.

Knight, G.E.O., *Intimate Glimpses of Mysterious Tibet and Neighbouring Countries*. New Delhi, India: Asian Educational Services, 1992.

Galland, China, *The Bond Between Women: A Journey to Fierce Compassion.*, New York: Riverhead Books, 1998.

LePage, Victoria, *Shambhala: The Fascinating Truth Behind the Myth of Shangri-La*. Wheaton, Ill.: Quest Books, 1996.

Matthiesson, Peter, *The Snow Leopard*. New York: The Viking Press, 1978.

Pemba, Tsewang, *Young Days In Tibet*. London: Jonathan Cape, 1957.

Sanday, John, *The Kathmandu Valley: Jewel of the Kingdom of Nepal*. Lincolnwood, Ill.: Passport Books, 1995.

Philosophical and Doctrinal

Bhikkhu, Buddhadasa, *Heartwood of the Bodhi Tree: The Buddha's Teaching on Voidness.* Boston: Wisdom Publications, 1994.

Burtt, E.A. (ed.), *The Teachings of the Compassionate Buddha: Early Discourses: The Dhammapada, and Later Writings,* 14th printing. New York: The New American Library, 1955.

Bhattacharyya, Benoytosh, *An Introduction to Buddhist Esotericism:* Varanasi, India: The Chowkhamba Sanskrit Series Office, 1964.

Chang, Garma C.C. (trans.), *The Hundred Thousand Songs of Milarepa,* Volumes 1 and 2. New Hyde Park, N.Y.: University Books, 1962.

Conze, Edward, *Buddhist Meditation.* New York: Harper & Row, Publishers, 1969.

Conze, Edward (trans.), *Buddhist Scriptures.* Middlesex, England: Penguin Books, 1959.

David-Neel, Alexandra, and Lama Yongden, *The Secret Oral Teachings in Tibetan Buddhist Sects.* San Francisco: City Lights Books, 1967.

Evans-Wentz, W.Y. (ed.), *The Tibetan Book of the Dead: or The After-Death Experiences on the Bardo Plane, According to Lama Kazi Dawa-Samdup's English Rendering.* New York: Oxford University Press, 1980.

Evans-Wentz, W.Y. (ed.), *The Tibetan Book of the Great Liberation: or The Method of Realizing Nirvana Through Knowing the Mind.* London: Oxford University Press, 1954.

Evans-Wentz, W.Y. (ed.) *Tibetan Yoga and Secret Doctrines.* London: Oxford University Press, 1973.

Evans-Wentz, W.Y. (ed.), *Tibet's Great Yogi Milarepa: A Biography from the Tibetan.* London: Oxford University Press.

Ghose, Sudhin N, *Tibetan Folk Tales and Fairy Stories.* New Delhi, India: Rupa & Company, 1986.

Govinda, Lama Anagarika, *Foundations of Tibetan Mysticism.* New Delhi, India: B. I. Publicatons, PVT, Ltd., 1977.

Govinda, Lama Anagarika, *The Way of the White Clouds: A Buddhist in Tibet.* New Delhi, India: B.I. Publications, 1977.

Guenther, Herbert V. (trans.), *The Life and Teachings of Naropa, Translated From the Original Tibetan With a Philosophical Commentary Based on the Oral Transmission.* London: Oxford University Press, 1963.

Gyatsu, Tenzin, The Fourteenth Dalai Lama, *An Introduction to Buddhism.* New Delhi, India, Secretariat of H.H. the Dalai Lama, n.d.

McKeon, Richard (ed.), *The Basic Works of Aristotle.* New York: Random House, 1941.

Piburn, Sidney (ed.), *The Nobel Peace Prize and the Dalai Lama,* Ithaca: Snow Lion Publications, 1990, p. 40.

Prabhavananda, Swami, and Frederick Manchester, (trans.), *The Upanishads: Breath of the Eternal.* New York: Mentor Books, 1975.

Rangdrol, Tsele Natsok, *The Mirror of Mindfulness.* Boston: Shambhala Publications, 1989.

Snellgrove, David (trans. and ed.), *The Nine Ways of Bon, Excerpts from gZi-brjid.* London: Oxford University Press, 1967.

Sprung, Mervyn (trans.), *Lucid Exposition of the Middle Way: the Essential Chapters From the Prasannapada of Candrakirti.* London: Routledge & Kegan Paul, 1979.

Thurman, Robert A.F. (trans.), *The Tibetan Book of the Dead: Liberation Through Understanding in the Between.* New York: Bantam Books, 1993.

Tsongkapa, *The Principal Teachings of Buddhism.* Howell, N.J.: Classics of Middle Asia, 1988.

Trungpa, Chogyam, *Cutting Through Spiritual Materialism.* Boston: Shambhala Publications, 1973.

Trungpa, Chogyam, *Shambhala, The Sacred Path of the Warrior.* Boston: Shambhala Publications, 1984.

Whitney, William Dwight (trans.), *Atharva-Veda*, Volumes 1, 2. Delhi: Motilal Banarsidass, 1971.

Index

QUEST BOOKS
are published by
The Theosophical Society in America
Wheaton, Illinois 60189-0270,
a branch of a world organization
dedicated to the promotion of the unity of
humanity and the encouragement of the study of
religion, philosophy, and science, to the end that
we may better understand ourselves and our place in
the universe. The Society stands for complete
freedom of individual search and belief.
For further information about its activities,
write, call 1-800-669-1571, or consult its Web page:
http://www.theosophical.org

The Theosophical Publishing House
is aided by the generous support of
THE KERN FOUNDATION,
a trust established by Herbert A. Kern
and dedicated to Theosophical education.